D0824728

Primary Sources of World Cultures™

ARGENTINA

A PRIMARY SOURCE CULTURAL GUIDE

Theodore Link
and Rose McCarthy

The Rosen Publishing Group's
PowerPlus Books™
New York

Published in 2004 by The Rosen Publishing Group, Inc.
29 East 21st Street, New York, NY 10010

First Edition

Library of Congress Cataloging-in-Publication Data
Link, Theodore.
Argentina: a primary source cultural guide/ by Theodore Link and Rose McCarthy.— 1st ed.
     p. cm. — (Primary sources of world cultures)
Summary: An overview of the history and culture of Argentina and its people including the geography, myths, arts, daily life, education, industry, and government, with illustrations from primary source documents.
Includes bibliographical references and index.
ISBN 0-8239-3997-9 (library binding)
1. Argentina—Juvenile literature. [1. Argentina.] I. McCarthy, Rose. II. Title. III. Series.
F2808.2.L56 2003
982—dc21
                                                                                  2003003800

Manufactured in the United States of America

Cover Images: Tango dancers (*right*), Casa Rosado in Buenos Aires (Government House) (*center*), Cueva de las Manos (cave paintings dated between 10,000 and 9000 BC) (*background*)

Photo credits: Cover (background), 44, 52, 62, 67 (bottom), 69, 72 (bottom), 76, 77 (bottom), 105, 118 (top left), 119 © Matton Images; cover (middle) © Max and Bea Hunn/D. Donne Bryant; cover (bottom) © Santiago Porter/Clarin Contenidos; pp. 3, 118, 120 © 2002 GeoAtlas; pp. 4 (top), 10, 48 (top) © Superstock; pp. 4 (middle and bottom), 13 (bottom), 15, 16, 18, 27 (bottom), 34, 35, 43, 45, 47, 67 (top), 108 (bottom) © Focus AR/ Matton Images; pp. 5 (top), 22, 30 (top and bottom), 64 © Bettmann/Corbis; pp. 5 (middle), 56 © Agustin Beltrame/Clarin Contenidos; pp. 5 (bottom), 103 © ImageState; p. 6 © Carlos Goldin/Focus/D. Donne Bryant; pp. 7, 37, 109 © Getty Images; p. 8 © Georg Gerster/Photo Researchers, Inc.; p. 9 © Tony Morrison/South American Pictures; pp. 11, 118 (bottom left) © Tim Davis/Photo Researchers, Inc.; p. 12 © Kit Houghton/Corbis; p. 13 (top) © Yann Arthus-Bertrand/Corbis; p. 14 © Will and Deni Mcintyre/Photo Researchers, Inc.; p. 17 © Tibor Bognar/Corbis; p. 19 © Don Boroughs/The Image Works; pp. 20, 28, 29, 104 (bottom) © Chris R. Sharp/D. Donne Bryant; p. 21 (top) © Peter Oxford/Nature Picture Library; p. 21 (bottom) © Jeff Foott/Nature Picture Library; p. 23 © Dagli Orti/Museo de Universidad la Plata Argentina/Art Archive; pp. 24 (top), 82, 106 © Hulton Archive/Getty Images; p. 24 (bottom) © Mary Evans Picture Library; pp. 25, 26 (bottom), 27 (top), 31, 63, 81, 110 © Archivo General de la Nacion; p. 26 (top) © Dagli Orti/Museo Historico Nacional Buenos Aires/Art Archive; pp. 32 (top), 60, 102 © Larry Luxner; p. 32 (bottom) © Patrick Zachmann/Magnum Photos; p. 33 (top) © AFP Photo; p. 33 (bottom) © Gabriel Piko/Cover/The Image Works; pp. 36, 99 © Ferdinando Scianna/ Magnum Photos; p. 38 (top) © Joaquin Salvador Lavado, Quino; p. 38 (bottom), 90 © Stuart Cohen/The Image Works; p. 40 (top) © Mireille Vautier/Woodfin Camp and Associates; p. 40 (bottom) © Robert Frerck/Woodfin Camp and Associates; p. 41 © Pedro Martinez/South American Pictures; p. 42 © Luis Martin/D. Donne Bryant; pp. 46, 55 (bottom), 66, 108 (top) © National Geographic; p. 48 (bottom) © Northwind Pictures; p. 50 © Hulton-Deutsch Collection/Corbis; pp. 51, 85, 87 (bottom) © Katsuyoshi Tanaka/Woodfin Camp and Associates; p. 53 © Joe Viesti/Viesti Associates, Inc.; p. 54 © Daniel Luna/Clarin Contenidos; pp. 55 (top), 59, 79 © Stuart Franklin/Magnum Photos; p. 57 © Peter Wilson/Axiom; pp. 58, 68 © Frank Nowikowski/South American Pictures; p. 61 © Bojan Breceli/Corbis; p. 65 © AKG Photo; pp. 70, 75 (top) © Private Collection José Antonio Berni/Christie's Images, Ltd.; pp. 71, 118 (top right) © Bachmann/Photri, Inc.; p. 72 (top) © Dagli Orti/Museo de Universidad la Plata Argentina/Art Archive; p. 73 © Nicolas Sapieha/Art Resource; p. 74 © Rights of Reproduction Fundacion Pan Klub, Museo Xul Solar/Christie's Images, Ltd.; p. 75 (bottom) © Corbis Sygma; p. 77 (top) © Hubert Stadler/Corbis; p. 78 © Stone/Getty Images; p. 80 © Doug McKinlay/Axiom; p. 83 © Enrique Shore/Cover/The Image Works; p. 84 © Marion Kalter/AKG London; p. 86 © Photofest; p. 87 (top) © Eugene Maynard/Redferns/ Retna Ltd.; pp. 88, 89 © South American Pictures; p. 91, 96 © Robert Fried; p. 93 © Photodisc/Getty Images; p. 94 © Fernanda Rocha; p. 95 © Brauner/ Stockfood; p. 97 © Fabio Cuttica/Constrasto; p. 98 © D. Donne Bryant; p. 100 © Mike Harding/South American Pictures; p. 101 (top) © Daniel Garcia/AFP Photo; p. 101 (bottom) © Allsport UK/Allsport/Getty Images; p. 104 (top) © Chris Sharp/South American Pictures; p. 107 © Earl and Nazima Kowall/Corbis; p. 111 © Hugo Scotte/Imagenlatina; p. 121 © Michael and Patricia Fogden/Corbis.

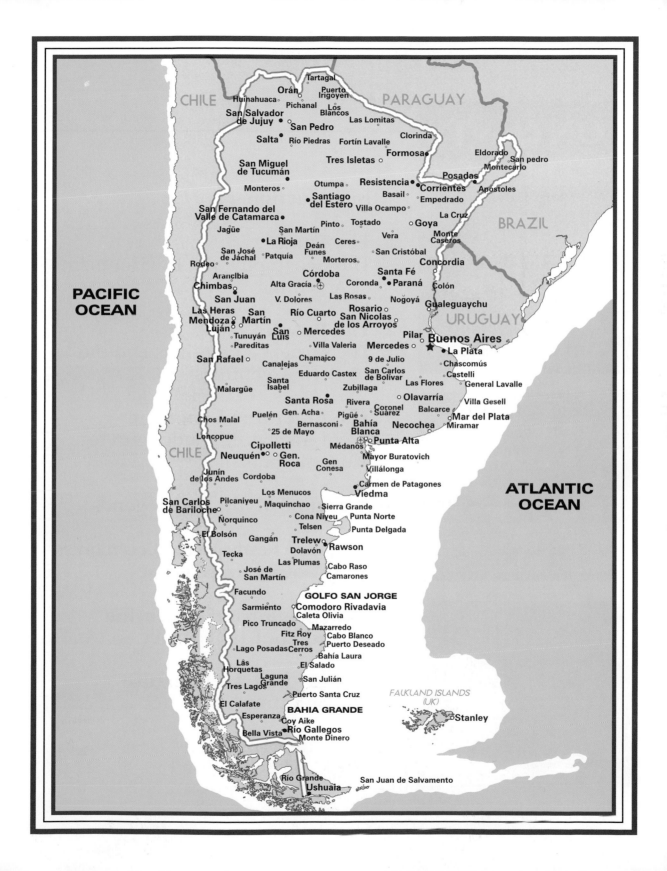

CONTENTS

INTRODUCTION

Argentina makes up most of South America's southern region, with tropical forests in the north eventually tapering down to the subantarctic southern reaches. The pampas, vast plains of fertile grasslands, cover much of central Argentina. The imposing Andes mountains form the western border, and a sweeping Atlantic coastline lies to the east. Abandoned Jesuit missions dot the humid north, stately colonial cities occupy the country's heartland, and a few towns and cities brave the desolate beauty of harsh Patagonia.

The vibrant port of Buenos Aires is the federal capital of Argentina as well as its cultural center. Livestock and grain grown on the pampas brought riches to the country during the end of the nineteenth century, and Argentines built a city that they hoped would rival the great cities of Europe. The city boasts a world-class opera house, one of the widest avenues in the world, and neighborhoods of opulent mansions. Working-class people of Buenos Aires invented the tango, the sultry national music and dance form of Argentina that has gained recognition across the world.

A gaucho *(left)* rides through the streets of Córdoba. Gauchos, the cattlemen of Argentina, are known for leading a simple life on the pampas, or plains. Today, the word "gaucho" is synonymous with nobility of heart. Located on the eastern edge of Patagonia's ice caps in Los Glaciares National Park, Mount Fitzroy *(above)* is a granite peaked mountain that reaches a height of 11,073 feet (3,375 meters).

Argentina's capital city, Buenos Aires, is a port city located on the Río de la Plata. It has been the gateway to Argentina for centuries. The city is home to 3 million people. The people of Buenos Aires are called *porteños*, literally meaning "people of the port." There is no main focal point to the city, no dominating monuments, or large monoliths. Instead, there are many intimate neighborhoods. Glass skyscrapers, nineteenth-century Victorian houses, tango bars, and antique shops all reside together. The city has been described as one of the most sophisticated cities in South America with a buzz and excitement like that of New York City.

To many Argentines, Buenos Aires represents the heart of the country. Many of the city's residents rarely travel further than the surrounding pampas and coastline. They consider the rest of Argentina sleepy and unsophisticated. The dynamic capital overshadows much of the beauty and rich culture of the rest of the country. Argentines' enduring respect for the gauchos who tamed the pampas is the best reminder that the country extends beyond Buenos Aires. The heart of Argentina's wine industry is in the foothills of the Andes in the western province of Mendoza. Timber from the northern forests was used to build the railroads and power lines that now extend into forbidding southern Patagonia. To the far south, ships sail through the Beagle Channel and the Strait of Magellan on their way around the tip of South America.

The nation gave the world the writing of Jorge Luis Borges and the jazzy tango music of Astor Piazzolla, but

most Americans are more familiar with Argentina's darker side. The country has failed to solve the political conflicts and economic instability persisting throughout much of the twentieth century. Many Argentines still adore the memory of the glamorous Eva (Evita) Perón. She helped her husband, President Juan Domingo Perón, support the rights of the working class, but his policies brought the economy to the brink of ruin. A bloody military regime waged the Dirty War against its own people from 1976 to 1983. More recently, the nation reached an economic crisis in 2001 and has dissolved into financial chaos. Hopefully, the resourceful Argentine people will come together to resolve the country's crises and bring back some of the grandeur of its proud past.

Argentina's temperate climate and the high mineral content of the soil are ideal for growing grapes. The continental climate has four distinct seasons without extreme temperatures, which enable grapes to mature. Since Argentina's vineyards are at a higher elevation than most (1,500 to over 5,000 feet [457–1,524 m]), they receive very little rainfall and must be irrigated.

THE LAND

1

The Geography and Environment of Argentina

Argentina is the second largest country in South America after Brazil. Thick at its top and middle and gradually tapering southward, Argentina's land area of 1.07 million square miles (2.8 million square kilometers) makes it the eighth largest nation in the world. It is about the size of the United States east of the Mississippi River, 2,170 miles (3,500 km) long and 868 miles (1,400 km) across its widest point.

Argentina rests at the southeastern end of South America. The imposing Andes mountains form the western border with Chile. Bolivia and Paraguay border its northern regions, while Brazil and Uruguay lie to the northeast. The island of Tierra del Fuego, shared with Chile, makes up Argentina's southern tip. The curving 2,936-mile (4,989-km) coastline travels along the Atlantic Ocean to the east, down to the southern tip of the country at Tierra del Fuego.

There are six major regions in Argentina. They include the Pampas, Mesopotamia, Chaco, the High Desert, the Cuyo, and Patagonia.

Pampas

Argentina's Pampas region covers most of the country's center. Farmers take advantage of its deep, fertile topsoil and vast plains, making the Pampas Argentina's agricultural

View of Plaza San Martín in Córdoba, which is named after Argentina's great liberator *(left)*. Córdoba was once Argentina's center of arts and learning, where priests and scholars congregated. Ushuaia, the most southern city in the world *(above)*, is the capital of the province of Tierra del Fuego. The city is located on the border of the Beagle Channel, surrounded by Mounts Marial. The city is set in a landscape of mountains, sea, glaciers, and woods. Ushuaia, a popular site for skiing, mountaineering, and hiking, is the departure point for excursions to Antarctica.

Gauchos herd cattle on the pampas for wealthy land-owners. The gauchos' lives have changed. The large ranches where they work are now fenced in as more people settle on the plain. The surviving gauchos continue to mend fences, brand cattle, and round up herds.

heartland. Enormous herds of cattle graze on the *estancias* (ranches). The cattle once roamed freely, but today farmers have fenced in their pastures. The Pampas region is divided into two sections. The *pampa humeda* (humid pampa) lies to the east and is home to most of Argentina's agriculture. Cattle and fields of grain compete for space here. The *pampa seca* (dry pampa) lies to the west. This more sparsely settled area provides pasture for sheep and cattle. The flatlands become slightly more rugged closer to the Andes. Ancient mountain ranges break the landscape at the western edge. Other highlands are found near the eastern coastline. The tallest of these sierras is Cerro Tres Picos, rising to 4,065 feet (1,239 meters).

Argentina's capital, Buenos Aires, is located in the northeastern corner of the Pampas, where the Río de la Plata meets the Atlantic Ocean. It is a beautiful and bustling port. Three million people live in the city itself, the country's largest. About 45 percent (13 million) of all Argentines live in greater Buenos Aires. South of Buenos Aires, the Atlantic beaches and the resort town of Mar del Plata, draw millions of visitors every summer.

Mar del Plata is the most famous seaside resort of Argentina's Atlantic coast. The city is often referred to as "la Ciudad Feliz" (the happy city) or "la Perla del Atlántico" (the pearl of the Atlantic) because of its 29 miles (47 km) of gorgeous beaches and lush landscape.

Córdoba is Argentina's second largest city. Founded in 1573 on the pampa seca by the Spanish explorer Jerónimo Luis de Cabrera, it is home to 1,179,000 Argentines. Just northeast of the city, a saltwater lake, Laguna Mar Chiquita, boasts thermal baths and pristine wilderness areas. About 62 miles long (100 km) and 24 miles wide (40 km), Laguna Mar Chiquita is Argentina's largest lake.

Mesopotamia

Early explorers and settlers arriving in Argentina's northeastern corner named the area Mesopotamia, after the fertile river valley located in the ancient Persian Empire. Mesopotamia lies along the borders of Bolivia, Paraguay, Brazil, and Uruguay. The Paraná, Uruguay, and Iguaçú Rivers form its natural boundaries. Rivers and streams dominate

The yerba maté tree grows in Argentina, Uruguay, Paraguay, and southern Brazil. The leaves of the yerba maté are dried to make maté, a tealike beverage that is highly caffeinated. Maté is the national drink of Argentina. Gauchos depend on maté, which is served in a gourd and sipped through a straw called a bombilla.

The Iguaçú Falls are on the border of Argentina and Brazil, just east of the junction of the Iguaçú and Paraná Rivers, located in Iguaçú National Park. The Iguaçú Falls, named for the Guaraní word meaning "big water," consist of more than 275 falls over 200 feet (60 m) high.

the region, and much of it disappears under water during the rainy season.

Low hills and swamps cover Mesopotamia's southern end, where ranchers raise sheep, cattle, and horses. The northern end is a subtropical and extremely humid paradise of hardwood forests. Argentines here raise crops of fruit and yerba maté, a plant used to produce a tea-like beverage popular throughout the country. In the northernmost tip, a plateau rises above the valley. The Paraná River crashes its way through the stone at Iguaçú Falls, where 275 cascades drop water over 200 feet (60 m)! The region's largest city, Rosario, was once the second largest port in Argentina. Today the city is still a major grain port with a population just over one million people.

Chaco

Argentina's north central Chaco region is the southern section of South America's huge Gran Chaco. This wilderness of forests and savannas also runs through Bolivia, Paraguay, and Brazil. The area is made up of jungle plains, swamps, and palm groves to the east and dry savanna in the western end. The Río de la Plata basin runs through the Chaco, causing floods during the rainy season. Many smaller rivers in the region drain into sinkholes. The timber industry profits greatly from the hardwood forests along the Río de la Plata basin. Farmers use the cleared areas to grow maize or cotton. Cattle graze on the savannas.

High Desert

The Andes are the dominant feature of Argentina's northwestern high-desert region. Here, the Andes split into two parallel *cordilleras* (ranges). The Salta-Jujeña cordillera runs westward, while the Sierra Subandinas extends to the east. The northern mountains and southern altiplano (high plateau) make up the cold and dry

puna desert. A sparse population herds sheep, goats, and llamas in this unfriendly landscape.

The eastern end of the High Desert becomes more hospitable as the altitude decreases. A tropical mountain climate with mild winters makes it excellent farm country. Growers raise olives, citrus, sugarcane, vegetables, and tobacco. The vast salt plains that make up the Salinas Grandes extend across the region's southeastern lowlands.

The Cuyo

Just south of the High Desert is the Cuyo, Argentina's central western region. The towering Andes meet in a single massive range. Many of the mountains here rise above 20,000 feet (6,100 m). At 22,834 feet (6,960 m), Aconcagua is the highest peak in the Western Hemisphere. The altiplano here is mostly desert and contains vast mineral wealth. Deposits of copper, lead, and uranium fuel the Cuyo's mining industry.

Rivers cascade down the mountains, turning the lower elevations into lush farmland. Some of the soil is used for growing citrus, while the larger part goes to vineyards. The region's valleys form the heart of Argentina's wine industry. The Cuyo

The Salinas Grandes in the Jujuy province are massive salt deposits located at 11,050 feet (3,368 m) above sea level. This semiarid and desolate area is characterized by its hot, dry climate. A relatively small number of people live in the region. A major portion of the territory in Jujuy is covered by the altiplano. The Guaytayoc Lagoon, also located in this province, has a high concentration of salt which is solid in some parts. The major economic activity in the Jujuy province is mining.

Aconcagua is referred to as "techo de America" (roof of America) because it is the highest mountain in the Western Hemisphere. Aconcagua is an eroded and dormant volcano in the dry region of the Andes. The high elevation, unpredictable weather, and extreme cold make it dangerous to climb.

is occasionally plagued by earthquakes caused by the grinding of the tectonic plates that make up the earth's crust. The region contains a fault where two of these plates meet. Mendoza, the largest city in the Cuyo, was almost destroyed by an earthquake in 1861. Completely rebuilt, the city is now home to about 150,000 people.

Patagonia

The tundra, glaciers, and mountains of Patagonia make up Argentina's southern region. Argentina's share of Patagonia covers about 1,200 square miles (3,108 square kilometers), a quarter of the country's landmass. The region extends from the Río Colorado to the very tip of South America.

The region's northern portion is made up of rolling plains and plateaus, offering plentiful grazing space for sheep. The Andes in western Patagonia are lower than those in the Cuyo. Forests cover the lower slopes of many peaks. Lakes and glaciers are scattered throughout the region. Northwestern Patagonia is often called Argentina's lake district. The area covers a 300-mile (500-km) stretch of lakes, including Lago Amutui Quimei, Lago Aluminé, and Laguna Blanca. These lakes are surrounded by national parks where visitors can hike, camp, or fish.

Imposing, fossil-rich cliffs mark the Atlantic coastline to the east. The region's major port, Comodoro Rivadavia, is a trading point for Patagonia's oil and natural

gas fields. Eastern Patagonia also boasts the lowest point in South America. The Salinas Chicas on the Península Valdés are at 130 feet (40 m) below sea level.

Farther south, Patagonia's plains turn into stark, rocky tundra, while glaciers and canyons break the landscape. The Parque Nacional Los Glaciares in the southwest protects many of the glaciers that make up the 250-mile-long (400-km) Patagonian ice cap. To the far south, the Strait of Magellan separates mainland Argentina from the large island of Tierra del Fuego. Argentina and Chile each own half of the island. Ushuaia on the Argentine side is its largest city. It has about fifty thousand citizens and is the world's southernmost city. It served as a prison town during the early twentieth century.

Perito Moreno Glacier in the Patagonia region was formed 30,000 years ago. It reaches a height of 197 feet (60 m). The 3.1-mile (5-km) front stretches across Lake Argentino. The Perito Moreno Glacier is the only glacier in the world still growing. It moves an average of 6.5 feet (2 m) per day. Falling snow accumulates faster than it melts and compresses behind the glacier to force it down the mountain. The glacier's blue color is caused by oxygen trapped in the snow. Dirt and mud cling to the glacier as it moves forward.

The Patagonian desert has an average temperature of 45°F (7°C). It is located between the Andes and the Atlantic Ocean. This region was a lush rainforest which became a petrified forest when it was covered with ashes from the volcanic action that formed the Andes. Native American tribes, who later inhabited the area, created cave painting. The Patagonian desert is mined for gas, coal, and oil.

Climate and Environment

Argentina's seasons are opposite those in the Northern Hemisphere. Winter lasts from May to July, while December, January, and February are summer months. Small tropical areas exist in Mesopotamia and parts of the Chaco. Temperatures as high as 113°F (45°C) have been recorded in these steamy regions near the Tropic of Capricorn. The high Andes and Patagonia stay cold and dry. Average winter temperatures in these areas hover around 32°F (0°C). Winds often rake across the high Andes, contributing to the region's barren landscape. Storms constantly slam into southern Patagonia, and winds of up to 200 mph batter the region. The Atlantic Ocean moderates most of the country's climate. The weather throughout much of the Pampas is therefore pleasant, though it is occasionally swept by windstorms. Buenos Aires averages temperatures between 63°F and 85°F (17°C to 29°C) during the summer months and 42°F to 57°F (6°C to 14°C) in the winter.

Northern Argentina receives about 60 inches (150 centimeters) of rain every year. Heavy summer rains often cause flooding in the Chaco and Mesopotamia. The

Pampas and Buenos Aires get about 37 inches (94 cm) of rain a year. Little rain falls in the far south and high Andes. Mendoza, in the Cuyo, receives only about 7 inches (18 cm) of rain annually.

Argentina is trying to address environmental issues. The country has taken a leadership role in voluntarily setting goals for reducing the emission of greenhouse gases. The winds blowing across the plains that surround the country's most populous region help disperse pollution. Still, the country faces losing its woodlands in the Chaco and Mesopotamia regions to logging. In northern Patagonia, overgrazing and poor crop management have exhausted some farmlands.

These icebergs are located in the Santa Cruz province. Icebergs are chunks of ice that have broken off of glaciers. On the southwestern side of Argentina, there are more than 300 glaciers, many of which are in Santa Cruz's Glaciers National Park. An UNESCO World Heritage Site, this national park forms the Patagonian Continental Ice Field. Here, thirteen glaciers descend on the Atlantic side to flow into the Viedma and Argentino Lakes.

Plants and Animals

Argentina's vast area provides a home for a wealth of wildlife. Mesopotamia and the Chaco, with areas of dense jungle, have the greatest variety of species. Hardwoods

The ombú tree is a giant treelike weed found on the pampas. The tree's poisonous sap and the fire-resistant trunk protect it against the dry climate and grazing cattle. The ombú tree is called the Lighthouse of the Pampas for the shade it provides the gauchos.

like rosewood and jacaranda grow along the riverbanks, while palm groves are plentiful throughout both regions.

Few native plants besides grasses and shrubs grow on the pampas. The only native tree on the pampas is actually a tall weed called the ombú. Estancia owners imported drought-resistant trees such as sycamores and acacias and planted them in rows to serve as windbreaks. Conifers such as fir, cypress, pine, and cedar grow in the Andean foothills. Citrus groves, sugarcane, and yerba maté thrive in the western valleys. The high Andes support only evergreen shrubs and some grasses. Patagonia's vegetation is sparse, with grasses, herbs, and shrubs making up most of the region's plant life. Conifers grow in the northern mountains of the region. Little grows at Patagonia's southern tip but lichen.

In the hot, marshy north, monkeys, raccoons, anteaters, and tapirs survive on diets of insects and vegetation. Predators such as jaguars and pumas compete for the smaller, plant-eating creatures. Alligators lie in wait underwater for their meals. More than four hundred kinds of birds live in the area around Iguaçú Falls. Flamingos, parrots, and hummingbirds are all common sights here and in the swampy Chaco.

Animals on the pampas mostly stay close to the ground. Burrowing rodents called vizcachas form large communities on the plains. The largest rodent in the

The Quebracho Tree

The hardy quebracho tree grows in Argentina's Chaco region. Quebracho trees grow about 65 feet (20 m) tall, but their trunks can measure 6 feet (2 m) in diameter. They take a hundred years to mature. The wood from the quebracho is very strong and does not decay for decades. The name itself comes from a phrase literally meaning "ax-breaker"! Argentines use its tough wood for everything from telephone poles to ceiling rafters.

"Armadillo" is the Spanish word for "small and armored." The hairy armadillo lives in the grasslands of Argentina, Bolivia, Chile, and Uruguay. Its armor consists of a section on the head, a narrow strip on the neck and ears, and a large section made of eighteen strips that covers the body. The armadillo's underbody is covered with long, bristly hairs.

world, the capybara, which can exceed 4 feet (1.2 m) in length, also lives on the pampas. Foxes and armadillos are common in the wilder regions. Partridges nest in the grasslands, while rheas, the American ostrich, pound across the soil. Many of these species also range across Patagonia. Alpacas, llamas, vicuñas, and guanacos—all relatives of the camel—roam the rugged mountain regions.

Many forms of fish and aquatic mammals are found off the coast. A type of dolphin called the dorado and pods of orcas are often seen off the coast. Inland fishermen catch bass and trout from the rivers and lakes. The more adventurous head for the ocean and try to catch the maguruyú, a massive fish that can weigh more than 200 pounds (90 kg). Sea lions raise their young on Patagonia's cold beaches. The Punto Tombo Reserve off the southern coast boasts the largest number of penguins outside Antarctica. Twelve other national parks throughout the country protect Argentina's diverse wildlife.

These are southern elephant seals on the beach of the Valdés Peninsula. Hunted for oil during the nineteenth and early twentieth centuries, the southern elephant seals are now protected by the Convention for the Conservation of Antarctic Seals. An estimated 600,000 seals exist, but the numbers are still in decline. Scientists suspect it is because their food supply is dwindling.

THE PEOPLE

2

The Ancient Argentines and the Modern Argentines

Hunters from the north first settled in Argentina between 13,000 and 10,000 BC. Unlike the societies of Central America or parts of South America, Argentine Native Americans never established a lasting civilization or formed an empire. At least two dozen different cultural groups were spread out across the country. In the north and northwest, groups such as the Diaguita and Guaraní lived in small towns where they farmed. Tribes in the Pampas, Patagonia, and Tierra del Fuego led nomadic lives, hunting, fishing, and gathering food. The inhospitable southern regions were sparsely populated, averaging only a couple of people per square mile. In 1480, the Inca began extending their empire into northern Argentina.

Juan Díaz de Solís, a Portuguese explorer working for the Spanish, led the first European expedition into Argentina in 1516. They sought a passage through South America to the Pacific. Solís sailed up the Río de la Plata and claimed the region for Spain. Local Native Americans captured and killed Solís and a group of his men. According to legend, they also ate the leader.

Argentine President Juan Perón and his wife, Eva, toured the streets of Buenos Aires after Perón was sworn in for his second term on June 9, 1952 *(left)*. In 1945, he joined a military group that overthrew the civilian government, and he became the vice president and minister of war. Perón was president of Argentina from 1946 to 1955, and again from 1973 to 1974. During Perón's presidency, he established the Third Position, a government he believed to be between communism and capitalism. A human face *(above)* is depicted on this vessel created by an Aguada Indian, circa AD 650 to 850.

Ferdinand Magellan (1480–1521) led the first expedition to sail around the world. In 1519, he left Seville with five ships to find a trade route through the Americas to the East Indies. Although he died on an island in the Pacific Ocean, his crew continued the journey, returning to Seville on September 8, 1522, with eighteen crew members, four East Indians, and one ship.

In 1520, Ferdinand Magellan sailed along the coast of Argentina and left the first accounts of Tierra del Fuego. Sebastian Cabot established a small settlement in 1527, but hostile Native Americans quickly destroyed it. Pedro de Mendoza founded the first significant colony in 1536. Fifteen hundred people settled at the mouth of the Río de la Plata. Mendoza called the town Santa María de los Buenos Aires. Local Querendí warriors led devastating attacks against the Spaniards. Facing starvation and illness, the colonists abandoned the settlement.

The Spanish gave up on Argentina's harsh coast. Instead, during the second half of the sixteenth century, conquistadores led groups of settlers over land into the northwestern portion of the country. They founded Argentina's oldest cities, including Mendoza, Tucumán, Córdoba, and many others. The new communities thrived, largely because of exploitation of Native American labor. In some areas, the Spanish supported the *encomienda* system. Native Americans worked for an important figure called the *encomiendero*. In return for their labor, he was supposed to educate them as Christians. Under another system called the *mita*, Native Americans

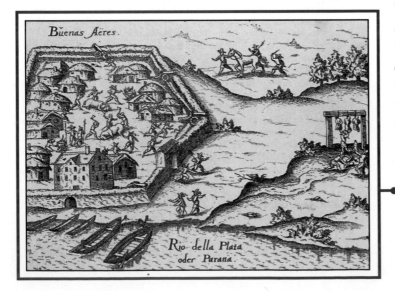

Illustration of Spanish conquistadors overrunning Buenos Aires. They slaughtered the animals and hung natives of the indigenous tribes. In 1515, Juan Díaz de Solís and his crew were the first to try to explore the Rio de la Plata. Upon landing, he and his crew were ambushed and killed.

contributed a certain amount of work to the colonial authorities. Native populations declined rapidly because of abuse, conflicts with the Spanish, and disease. The Spaniards began purchasing African slaves near the end of the sixteenth century as a source of cheap labor.

In 1580, Juan de Garay founded Buenos Aires at the mouth of the Río de la Plata. Unlike Mendoza's attempt, Garay's settlement survived. It grew slowly, however, because the Spanish did not permit free trade in the port. Residents began smuggling to avoid high prices for Spanish goods. By the eighteenth century, the town prospered because of smuggling. In 1702, the Spanish allowed the port to be opened for slave trade with the British. Most slaves did not remain in Buenos Aires for long, but by 1778, slaves and free Afro-Argentines made up 30 percent of the city's population.

By the beginning of the nineteenth century, Spain's empire was weakening. In 1806, British forces

Mistaken Identity

Early Spanish explorers hoped to make their fortune in Argentina. They named the newly discovered land for *argentum*, the Latin word for silver. Although Argentina has many natural resources, it has very little gold or silver! Nonetheless, the Argentines have kept their country's mistakenly bestowed name to this day.

A document by Juan de Garay, founder of Buenos Aires, outlined the division of the native population. The importance of Buenos Aires to the Spanish was its strategic location as a port with access to the interior of South America.

A watercolor illustration from the nineteenth century depicts the Congress of the United Provinces assembled in Tucumán. At this meeting, Argentina declared its independence from Spain and the first constitution of the country was written.

invaded Buenos Aires. The Spanish viceroy and his troops fled. Argentine forces ousted the British and also defeated another force that arrived in 1807. Their victory was a source of pride for the Argentines, and resentment of the Spanish sharpened. In 1808, Napoleon invaded Spain. As in many Latin American countries, Argentine nationalists took advantage of the chaos among the Spanish leaders. A *cabildo*, or town council, formed a junta to rule in place of the Spaniards on May 25, 1810. On July 9, 1816, the United Provinces of the Río de la Plata officially declared independence from Spain.

Argentina's independence could never be secure as long as the Spanish occupied South American territory. In a daring move, General José de San Martín led an army across the Andes to defeat the Spanish forces in Chile. He continued on to Lima, Peru, with a fleet of British and American ships. The Spanish surrendered with no resistance in 1822. San Martín, Argentina's national hero, retired and went into exile in France.

The Record of Independence declared by the Congress of the United Provinces was written in both Spanish and Quechua, the language of the Quechua Indians. Early in Argentina's struggle for independence from Spain, there were two political parties that bitterly disagreed about the type of government needed in the country. The Unitarios wanted a strong central government, while the Federales, or Federalists, favored local control.

The People: The Ancient Argentines and the Modern Argentines

Two political forces emerged in the young country. Bernardino Rivadavia led the Unitarios, who supported a strong central government in Buenos Aires. He tried to enact a constitution and attract immigrants to Argentina. His rule collapsed as a result of a disastrous war with Brazil from 1825 to 1828. The opposition party, the Federales, or Federalists, took power. The *caudillos*, large landowners of the pampas, supported the Federales. They did not want to have to answer to a central government. They were backed by a militia of gauchos, or Argentine cowboys.

A caudillo warlord named Juan Manuel de Rosas took power in 1829 and brought some stability to the country. Rosas refused to stay on as governor in 1832. He spent the next few years leading military campaigns against Native Americans in the south, exterminating thousands. In the meantime, his political allies gained power in Buenos Aires. Rosas took the office of governor once again, this time with nearly dictatorial authority.

Rosas brutally repressed any opponents. His spies, the police, and the military led a reign of terror. He had thousands tortured and killed, and many

Juan Manuel de Rosas (1793–1877) began his political career as leader of a band of gauchos who supported Federalism. In 1828, he became the Federalist leader. His government was tyrannical, aided by spies, propagandists, and the Mazorca (a secret political society of assassins).

people fled the country. Something as minor as wearing blue clothing—the color of the Unitarios—could bring about an arrest. Rosas distrusted foreigners, and his actions angered Europe and Argentina's neighbors. In 1852, his political opponents formed an army of Argentines, Uruguayans, and Brazilians led by Justo José de Urquiza. They easily defeated Rosas's forces.

Urquiza held a constitutional convention and declared himself president in 1853. Buenos Aires refused to recognize the authority of the new government. After a number of clashes, Buenos Aires accepted a slightly modified constitution in 1862, which strengthened the powers of the central government and made Buenos Aires the nation's capital. Bartolomé Mitre became the first president of a united Argentina.

In 1879, the minister of war, Julio Roca, led a campaign against the Native Americans of the Pampas and Patagonia. His forces exterminated or drove out any native groups they encountered. They forced the survivors onto reservations. Many people hailed Roca as a hero for opening the land to them for settlement and grazing. He served as president from 1880 to1886.

Argentina's golden age lasted from 1880 until the beginning of World War I. Exports of beef and grain made the country wealthy. A new rail network connected much of the country. Buenos Aires was transformed into a modern city, with public transportation, sewage and water systems, and other public works improvements. It became the economic and cultural center of Argentina, earning the nickname the Paris of South America. A wave of immigration began during the last decades of the nineteenth century. Half of these newcomers came

Photograph of La Boca Harbor in Buenos Aires taken in the early 1900s. Located on the Río de la Plata, La Boca Harbor was where immigrants arriving from Europe landed in the 1900s. Today, it is known as the district of artists.

The People: The Ancient Argentines and the Modern Argentines

Immigrants arriving in Buenos Aires. At the beginning of the twentieth century, Argentina was one of the wealthiest countries in Latin America. Foreign investment and immigrant workers helped to boost the economy. During the first decades of the 1900s, Argentina had a larger immigrant population than the United States.

from Italy and a quarter came from Spain, but Poles, French, Swiss, Germans, Russians, Welsh, English, and Middle Easterners all hoped to make their fortunes in Argentina as well. By 1915, foreigners made up nearly a third of Argentina's population.

Even during these prosperous times, economic and political troubles plagued the country. Much of the wealth and power remained in the hands of the conservative elite. Economic growth led to inflation that hurt poor Argentines. Workers began to organize into unions and clamor for a voice in the government.

In 1916, Hipólito Yrigoyen of the Radical Party became president. He deposed the wealthy ruling class from power but continued its pattern of repression. Workers led massive strikes in 1919. The army brutally put down the protests, opening fire on strikers during a bloody *Semana Trágica*, or tragic week. These government actions did not end labor unrest.

The Radical Party controlled the government until 1930. The Great Depression crippled Argentina, and a military coup brought a new regime to power. It resulted in an unstable and corrupt government that was overturned by another military coup in 1943.

This photograph shows President Juan Perón and his wife, Eva, at a workers' rally, where workers demanded they run for reelection. Eva convinced her husband to help the lower class Argentines and actively distributed wealth to the poor. With the support of the people, Perón was able to secure his presidency.

Juan Domingo Perón began his rise to power during this period. He would become Argentina's most influential political figure.

Perón was immensely popular with labor unions and the *descamisados* (shirtless ones), or poor workers. Supported by his mistress Eva Duarte (known as Evita), whom he later married, he easily won the presidency in 1946. Argentines still remain divided on his achievements. Supporters cite that his social reforms dramatically improved life for workers. Evita tirelessly campaigned for her husband and the descamisados and helped women gain the right to vote. Perón's critics point out that he brutally suppressed and

This photograph of graffiti scrawled across a building in Vicente López was taken in 1973 after the return of Juan Perón to Argentina. When he became president in 1973, there was constant conflict between Perón's left and right wing supporters. As a result, terrorism increased and emergency decrees were enacted to restore public order.

Issued in 1955, this decree confirms the new provisional government. It was issued by the office of the National Executive when Perón was forced from office by a military takeover. The army reinstated Argentina's constitution of 1973, which returned the government to a multiparty democracy. However, the military was unable to revive the country's economy or deal with increased social and labor issues.

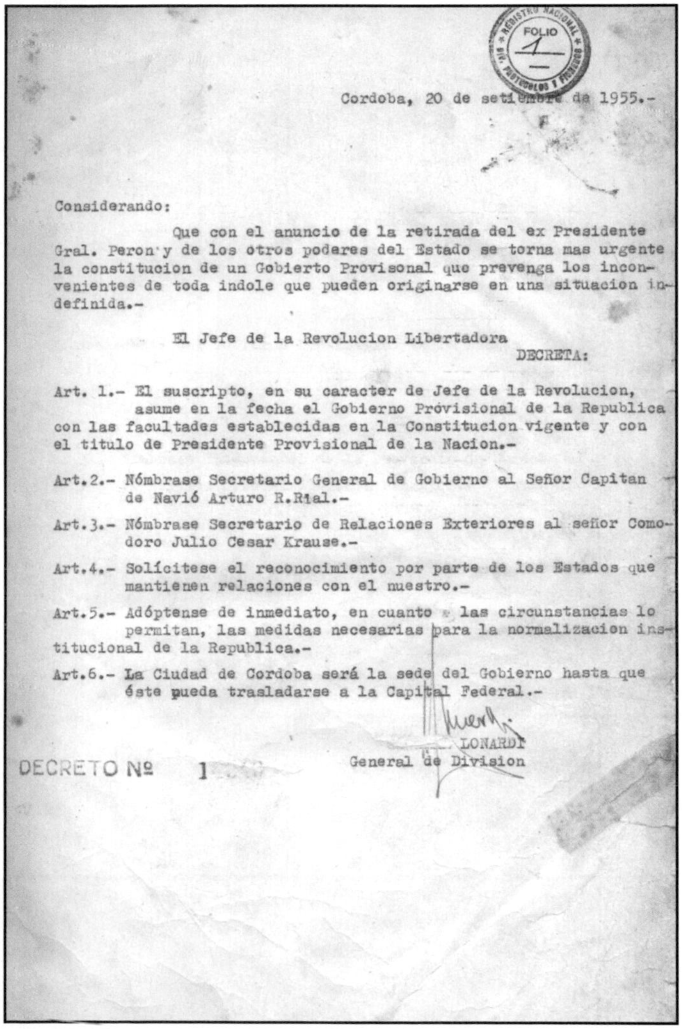

Cordoba, 20 de setiembre de 1955.-

Considerando:

Que con el anuncio de la retirada del ex Presidente Gral. Peron y de los otros poderes del Estado se torna mas urgente la constitucion de un Gobierno Provisonal que prevenga los inconvenientes de toda indole que pueden originarse en una situacion indefinida.-

El Jefe de la Revolucion Libertadora

DECRETA:

Art. 1.- El suscripto, en su caracter de Jefe de la Revolucion, asume en la fecha el Gobierno Provisional de la Republica con las facultades establecidas en la Constitucion vigente y con el titulo de Presidente Provisional de la Nacion.-

Art. 2.- Nómbrase Secretario General de Gobierno al Señor Capitan de Navió Arturo R.Rial.-

Art. 3.- Nómbrase Secretario de Relaciones Exteriores al señor Comodoro Julio Cesar Krause.-

Art. 4.- Solícitese el reconocimiento por parte de los Estados que mantienen relaciones con el nuestro.-

Art. 5.- Adóptense de inmediato, en cuanto las circunstancias lo permitan, las medidas necesarias para la normalizacion institucional de la Republica.-

Art. 6.- La Ciudad de Cordoba será la sede del Gobierno hasta que éste pueda trasladarse a la Capital Federal.-

LONARDI
General de Division

DECRETO Nº 1

censored any political opposition. Argentina's economy declined during Perón's second term, and some blame him for the country's financial ruin.

Because of these economic problems, support for Perón waned in the early 1950s. Evita Perón died of cancer in 1952, and another military coup sent Perón into exile. Short-lived military and civilian governments attempted to bring order to the country. But the economic plight worsened, and terrorist attacks by guerrilla groups plunged the country into chaos. Argentines began to support Perón's return, and he took office as president once again in 1973.

Perón died suddenly a year after taking power. His new wife, María Estela Martínez de Perón, known as Isabel, took the presidency. She was an incompetent leader, and the military deposed her in 1976. They ushered in one of the darkest periods of repression in Argentina's history.

A series of military juntas held power from 1976 to 1983. *El proceso,* "the process," also known as the Dirty War was launched. It attacked the guerrilla groups by targeting "subversive" or "antigovernment" Argentines. Between ten thousand and forty thousand

Chalk outlines in the Plaza de Mayo in Buenos Aires, represent the thousands of *desaparecidos*, people who were lost or killed during the Dirty War (1976–1983). On Thursdays, the Mothers of Plaza de Mayo, human rights activists, march around the chalk outlines of their relatives. Up to 30,000 people died or "disappeared" during the Dirty War.

people disappeared, taken into custody by officials and never seen again. The government would never give families any account of their fate. Union leaders, teachers, nuns, psychologists, journalists, lawyers, schoolchildren, doctors, and activists vanished. They were tortured and presumed dead.

Under military rule, the economy worsened. The junta looked for a new means of gaining the support of the Argentine people. In 1982, General Leopoldo Galtieri invaded the Falkland Islands, a nearby group of small islands held by the British. The Argentines call them the Islas Malvinas and believe that they should rightfully belong to Argentina. Galtieri did not believe that the British would fight to keep them. He was wrong. The British dealt the Argentine forces a crushing, embarrassing defeat. The junta stepped aside and allowed free elections in 1983.

Members of the Mothers of Plaza de Mayo assemble in front of the presidential palace on the Plaza de Mayo. In 1977, as a testimony to their courage, twelve women protested in the plaza while the junta was still in power. Several of them, including the founder of the group, "disappeared." Many men, women, and children have since joined demonstrations, carrying signs with photographs of their missing relatives.

Argentine soldiers are escorted by British soldiers after they surrendered on June 2, 1982, during the Falklands War. During the war, the British captured 10,000 Argentine prisoners, and all were released after the war. The defeat of Argentina discredited the military government and instigated a return to civilian rule in 1983.

Raúl Alfonsín of the Radical Party became the first president of the new democracy. Argentines rejoiced at the return of democratic freedoms. But Alfonsín and his successor, Carlos Saúl Menem, shocked people by pardoning many of the military leaders of the Dirty War. Since Alfonsín's election, Peronists and Radicals have vied for power. Neither party has succeeded in stabilizing the economy. In 2001, the value of the peso crashed during a deep recession. President Fernando de la Rúa of the Radical Party resigned amid riots. Peronist Eduardo Duhalde took the presidency in 2002, faced with a stagnant economy and social unrest.

President Duhalde's policies to stimulate the Argentine economy include limiting the open market and protecting local industry. However, his term as governor of the Buenos Aires province was plagued by accusation of corruption, and it is unclear how he will conduct business in Argentina's federal government.

Many immigrants left their countries for Argentina not knowing the language or culture. They came because Argentina had a healthy economy and was known to be receptive to immigrants. An Argentine newspaper called *Argentinisches Tageblatt*, which opposed German Nazism in the 1930s, helped German immigrants retain their language and culture.

Today's Argentines

Today, 37 million people live in Argentina. Eighty-five percent are of European origin. Native Americans (3 percent) and mestizos (12 percent), Argentines of mixed Native American and European blood, make up the remainder of the population.

About five hundred thousand Native Americans live in Argentina, although estimates vary. Their communities are concentrated in the northern, northwestern, and southern regions. Most of the country was only sparsely populated when the

The Proud Porteños of Buenos Aires

After Argentina won its independence, strife arose between the Federales of the country's interior and the Unitarios, who supported Buenos Aires as the seat of government. The balance of power was settled long ago. But cultural differences still remain between Buenos Aires and the rest of the country. Residents of Buenos Aires call themselves *porteños*, or "people of the port." Buenos Aires is, without question, the cultural as well as the political capital of Argentina. Porteños believe themselves more sophisticated, clever, and stylish than the "yokels" of the interior. Residents of the interior consider the porteños pretentious and are happy to avoid the fast pace of Buenos Aires.

A young Guaraní girl. The Guaraní tribes are spread throughout South America with an estimated 80,000 Guaraní inhabiting the lands of Argentina, Paraguay, Brazil, and Bolivia. The lifestyle of the Guaraní as wanderers of the forest is being threatened by the increasing destruction of forests by forestry companies.

Spaniards arrived. The small Native American population was further reduced by disease and the Spaniards' harsh treatment. As a result, Argentina has a smaller proportion of mestizos and Native Americans than its neighboring countries. Some Argentines still discriminate against the "indios," and many Native Americans live in poverty.

Afro-Argentines made up a significant amount of the population in the eighteenth and early nineteenth centuries. Half of San Martín's army was comprised of Afro-Argentine soldiers. Slaves could earn their freedom by serving in the military, and some Afro-Argentine men rose to the rank of officer. The proportion of Afro-Argentines dropped by the twentieth century, as they were greatly outnumbered by European immigrants. Many intermarried with the rest of the Argentine population.

During the late nineteenth centuries, a flood of immigrants brought greater diversity to Argentina. Most settled in cities, swelling the populations of Rosario, Santa Fe, and especially Buenos Aires, their point of arrival. A few, such as the Welsh and some central Europeans, formed communities in Patagonia. In recent years, other Latin Americans from neighboring countries have immigrated to Argentina, often illegally, to look for work.

THE ARGENTINE LANGUAGE

3

From Ancient Mapudungun to Modern Spanish

I f you are ever a guest in Argentina, your host may greet you with the friendly welcome of *¡Bienvenido a Argentina!* Argentines speak Spanish, or Castellano as they call it, referring to the Spanish region of Castile, where the language developed. It is a Romance language, sharing roots with French. The Romance languages began branching off from Latin in the ninth century. This family of languages adopted the Latin alphabet, also used by English and other European languages. Spanish spread across the globe beginning in the sixteenth century as the conquistadores traveled far and wide, lured by riches and fame. Today, more than 400 million people in at least forty-three countries speak fluent Spanish. It is the official language of most Central and South American countries.

A beginner first reading Spanish will find a few unfamiliar markings. A symbol called a tilde above an *n* changes its pronunciation. For example, in the word *mañana* (tomorrow), each *n* has its own sound: mahn-YAH-nah. Usually the stress falls on the last or second to last syllable of a word, but accent marks sometimes specify otherwise. *Sábado*

A large bookstore in Buenos Aires *(left)*. The literacy rate in Argentina is 96 percent, making the country the most literate in Latin America. Argentines place a strong emphasis on education, understanding that education is a requirement for success in a demanding economy. Front page of the January 6, 2002, issue of the Buenos Aires newspaper *Clarín* reads, "A New Economy Begins" *(above)*. The newspaper published twenty pages on the country's economy and how the devaluation of its currency would benefit the economy.

(Saturday) is pronounced SAH-bah-doh, and *fotografía* (photograph) is foh-toh-grah-FEE-ah. Queries begin with an inverted question mark, "¿", and end with a conventional question mark. Similarly, an exclamatory sentence begins with "¡" and ends in a regular exclamation point.

Letter pronunciation is more consistent than in English, with most having the same pronunciation in every context. Most vowels represent individual sounds rather than diphthongs. They are *a* as in "mama," *e* as in "mesa," *i* and *o* as in "mosquito," and *u* as in "June." Some consonants have only subtle distinctions from English, but a few sound significantly different. An *h* is always silent. The *j* sounds like a slightly guttural *h*, *qu* sounds like *k*, and every *r* is rolled. Unlike other Spanish speakers, Argentines pronounce *y* and *ll* with a *zh* sound as in "measure." The letters *x* and *z* are softer than in English, so *luz* (light) is pronounced LOOSS. The country of México is MEH-hee-koh.

A cartoon by well-known Argentine cartoonist Joaquín Salvador Quino depicts his most famous character, Mafalda *(above)*. Although his cartoons are childlike and involve school-age children, they were never meant for kids. The cartoons originally appeared in the editorial section of newspapers. People shop at a magazine stand *(left)*. Approximately 96 percent of Argentina's magazine distribution is through newsstands. The recession that has stalled Argentina's economy and a government-imposed tax on the cover price of magazines has negatively impacted sales.

Some grammatical situations in Spanish have no English equivalent. The word for "you" varies depending on the person being addressed and the circumstances. It may be either the formal *usted* or the familiar *vos*. The use of *vos* is unique to Argentines, as other Spanish speakers use the word *tú*. Most nouns are gendered in Spanish—generally, "feminine" nouns end in -*a*, "masculine" in -*o*. Words require different articles or adjective forms depending on gender, for example, *la tienda* (the store), or *el marcado* (the market).

Spanish spoken in Latin America is no longer identical to the Spanish of Spain. Dialects vary from one region to another, although Argentines have few problems communicating with other Spanish speakers. The differences arise mainly in the accents and idioms, much like the variances between British English and American English. Idiom also varies from one Argentine region to another. Argentine Spanish is peppered with *lunfardo*, a colorful slang most common in Buenos Aires. This mix of Italian and Spanish originated with working-class immigrants at the beginning of the twentieth century. Lunfardo

Vocabulary

Hello	Hola
Good day	Buenos días (more formal)
Good-bye	Adíos
Yes/No	Sí/No
Please	Por favor
Thank you	Gracias
Sorry!	Lo siento
I don't know.	No sé.
What is your name?	¿Como se llama usted?
My name is . . .	Me llamo . . .
I don't speak Spanish.	No hablo español.
Do you speak English?	¿Habla usted inglés?
What time is it?	¿Qué hora es?
Help!	¡Socorro!
I'm lost.	Estoy extraviado.
How much does it cost?	¿Cuánto cuesta?
Where is . . . ?	¿Donde está . . . ?
house	la casa
restaurant	el restaurante
bathroom	el baño
car	el carro
1	uno
2	dos
3	tres
4	cuatro
5	cinco

Argentines can be distinguished from other Latin Americans by their use of "Che" in conversation. Che, which has been incorporated into the Argentinean Spanish from the Mapuche, means "man." It is used as people in the U.S. might say "hey," "you know," or "eh." An Argentine would say "Che veni," meaning "Hey you, come here."

sometimes plays quirky games with words. For example, syllables might be reversed: *mujer* (woman) becomes *jumer*, *café* becomes *feca*.

Many English words come from Spanish origins, such as "mosquito," "banana," "barbecue," "ranch," "renegade," and "vanilla." Spanish also borrows from other languages. It has adopted many English words, especially terms related to technology and recent trends. Argentines think that *el internet*, taxis, and VCRs are *súper*.

Some words and place names in Argentine Spanish originated from languages spoken by Native Americans. More than two dozen indigenous languages existed in Argentina when the Spaniards first explored the country. Many of these languages survive today, although there is no significant movement to preserve native languages. A number of people speak fluent Guarani, Quechua, Toba, Wichi, and

Although Spanish is the official and most widely spoken language in Argentina, the government has mandated that children learn a second language. In most cases, English is the language of choice. This new law was implemented after the government recognized the importance of English in international business.

The Argentine Language: From Ancient Mapudungun to Modern Spanish

This photograph of Ona Indians dressed in guanaco skins was taken in the late nineteenth century. The last full-blooded Ona Indian died in 1977. The Ona Indians once inhabited Tierra del Fuego, land shared by Argentina and Chile. They survived by hunting, fishing, and gathering. The guanaco, a relative of the camel, provided the Ona with meat and fur to live.

Mapudungun, the language of the Mapuche tribe. Some languages, such as Pilagá or Mocoví, are only understood by a few thousand Native Americans. Others, such as Ona and Chané, are extinct or have only a handful of speakers.

Argentina's diverse array of immigrants also brought their own languages with them. Many learned Spanish but still clung to the languages of their countries of origin. During the nineteenth century and part of the twentieth, many immigrants came from England, Wales, Germany, France, and Italy, and they passed their languages on to the next generation. More recent arrivals speak Japanese, Arabic, and other African and Asian tongues.

ARGENTINE MYTHS AND LEGENDS

4

Argentina was once home to more than twenty distinct Native American cultures. Each tribe had its own set of established myths and folklore. Many tribes were devastated by war or disease during the nineteenth century, and their beliefs disappeared with them. Today, some Native Americans work to preserve their traditions, while others join Argentina's mainstream society and turn away from the old beliefs.

Gods and Spirits

Argentina's air is thick with the gods and spirits from various native traditions. These beings helped the shamans explain the workings of the world to the rest of their tribe. The Mbyá Guaraní tribe of Mesopotamia believed in a complex pantheon of supernatural beings. The Mbyá Guaraní deities began with Ñande Ru, who made the entire universe and every living creature. He created four other gods

An indigenous tribe that once inhabited the Tafi del Valle created a large monolith, called a *menhir (left)*. The 129 stone menhires that were found throughout the Tafi del Valle were moved to one location now known as Los Menhires Park where they are preserved. The menhires have an average height of 9.8 feet (3 m). One side of the stone is either carved or polished. A Guaraní shaman, or *paye*, wears his instruments used in ritual ceremonies *(above)*. The shaman is a religious leader said to possess supernatural powers to ward off evil and cure illness.

A portrait of a Toba Indian. Toba Indians are warlike hunters who live in the northern Argentina jungle of the Pilcomayo River. Not much is known about the Toba religion except that it involves revering the sun and rising moon. Toba Indians also believe that invisible spirits are responsible for sickness and misfortune.

to help him keep order in the world. Jakairá is the god of spring, responsible for renewal of life and the seasons. Karaí is the god of fire. He protects people from demons and spirits hiding in the dark. Ñamandú, god of the sun, ushers in every new day and infuses the world with energy. Tupã Ru Etê rules over rain and thunder. He brings the heavy summer rains to Mesopotamia.

Demons and spirits also play an important part in Mbyá Guaraní society. In the afterlife, the mighty demon Mbáé Pochy claims the spirits of criminals. He punishes guilty spirits forever, never letting them return to this world. The demon also torments villages with floods and sickness. Shamans must invoke Ñamandú's name in rituals to bring the sun and drive off the demon.

The Wichi tribe of the Chaco region shares the Mbyá Guaraní's fear of demons. The evil spirit Avacua is the most dreaded. This demon brings about lunar eclipses, making the moon disappear by breaking it into tiny bits. Avacua also causes sickness and sometimes death within a community. Villagers gather to drive the demon away whenever they detect its presence. They do this by shouting, drumming, lighting torches, and making as much noise as possible.

Animal Stories

Animals often play important roles in Argentina's folktales. In the northwestern plains and hills, people take care not to interfere with owls, who shepherd the souls of the dead to the cemetery. The Wichi have many tales about how various bird species came into being. Cardinals, known as Wosachut, had once been men who spent all of their days singing. An evil spirit named Tekwah heard their voices and became jealous. He transformed them into cardinals. Another popular tale is that of the woodpecker who was once a man called Siwok. Siwok was fishing when a very large fish swallowed him whole! Ijfwala the sun saw what happened and dried up the pond to save him. Siwok's soul flew out of the fish and became the woodpecker.

The Yamana tribe in Patagonia has a rich tradition of animal stories, most explaining animal behavior. According to one gory legend, the otter once had long legs. He also had five brothers-in-law who mocked him. The otter took revenge by killing four of his brothers-in-law. The fifth fought back and cut off his legs. Today, the otter has short legs and lives in underground burrows, afraid of being seen by other animals.

Many Argentines dislike disturbing the habits of cats. In some stories, cats deliver

This wooden figurine of a mottled owl was created by a Guaraní artisan. The Guaraní people consider themselves inseparable from nature and believe that the importance of land supersedes all else. Many of their legends and stories are centered around animals.

Incan figurines, found beside three Incan mummies at a burial site, depict two males and three llamas. The male statues may have been buried with the mummies as a gift to the gods. The Inca usually buried llama figurines with their dead to ensure the fertility of the Inca llama herds. Llamas were essential in the Incan culture, providing a form of transportation, meat, and leather.

water to the dead. Interrupting their travels could upset the spirits and bring despair to the person's household.

Other beasts walk the countryside undetected for much of the time. Argentines only worry about *lobisóns* (werewolves) when the moon is full. According to legend, the seventh son in a family—out of seven sons born in a row—is fated to become a lobisón. While a lobisón usually prefers to attack cattle rather than people during the full moon, Argentines take care to keep out of its way. They believe that anyone bitten by a lobisón in wolf form automatically becomes one.

Witches also once roamed Argentina's countryside. While the seventh son becomes a lobisón, the seventh daughter is born a witch. The legend of the seventh son or daughter created a panic during the early twentieth century. Families started abandoning these children and sometimes even killed them. The government stepped in during the 1920s, declaring that all of these children would be the godchildren of the president of Argentina. The president would attend the child's christening ceremony, presenting him or her with a gold medal. This helped end the practice, and the law is still in effect. Even today, the president attends the christening ceremony for a few seventh sons or daughters each year.

Other legends from the interior describe ordinary people caught up in miraculous events. The popular folk story of La Difunta Correa from the 1840s tells of a young woman named Deolinda Correa. "La Difunta" means "the deceased." One day she set out on foot with her infant son to find her husband's army battalion. She died of thirst and hunger in the desert of San Juan. A group of soldiers found her body a few days later. Her son was still alive, drinking her milk! A miracle was declared and shrines to

la Difunta Correa began appearing everywhere. Superstitious Argentines still ask her for help when they travel and leave offerings at her many shrines.

Modern Tales and Obsessions

Most of Argentina's population is descended from immigrants who settled in the country's cities during the late nineteenth century. Fresh from Europe with little connection to rural colonial folklore, they formed a unique urban mythology. To these *porteños*, gauchos still roam the plains, Evita will always be a saint, and the country is really much bigger than maps suggest.

Gauchos

The gauchos are one of Argentina's most enduring traditions. Little more than a memory, the culture of these Argentine cowboys persists in songs and stories. Gauchos are mestizo cattle workers who have lived on the pampas since the eighteenth century.

Difunta Correa followers have diverged from official Catholic doctrine. Although not a Catholic saint, Difunta Correa is revered and adored as if she were. Thousands of Catholics journey to her shrine in the hopes of receiving a miraculous gift. Argentines pray and often leave behind gifts in return for the granting of their favors. These items range from bottles of water to miniature models of cars and houses, to photographs of family members.

A photograph of a gaucho. The gauchos' courage and bravery are legendary and have been incorporated into the daily life of the people. To do a "gauchada" means to do a favor or solve a problem. The phrase refers to the gauchos' generosity and helpfulness.

Gauchos passed down their legendary horseback riding skills for generations. Many Argentines claim that the riders were so skilled that it was difficult to tell where the horse ended and the gaucho began.

Gauchos arrived on the unsettled pampas during the 1700s, where they captured and tamed wild horses. They used the horses to gather herds of wild cattle. Life on the pampas was hard, and the gauchos gained a reputation for toughness. They spent their days in the saddle, inventing games to help them improve their riding skills. In one test of skill, they rode their horses through a gauntlet of other gauchos. Those in the gauntlet tried to snare the horse's hoofs with rope loops, causing it to stop short and pitch the rider forward. The gaucho who could land on his feet with reins in hand was declared the winner.

Most gauchos owned little apart from a horse and saddle. They hunted with lassos and *boleadoras*, a weapon made up of three stones connected together by leather thongs. The gauchos threw these at an animal's feet, causing it to stumble. They made their own clothing from cured hides. Their only tools were knives, and they spent their nights rolled up in their ponchos against the cold. They sold the hides of

Indians hunted guanacos on the plains of Argentina 10,000 years ago. They relied heavily on their fur and meat. Guanacos were portrayed in canyon cave paintings as well as in woodcuts. Once overhunted, guanacos now thrive in protected areas.

wild cattle for tobacco, rum, and yerba maté. During the nineteenth century, ranchers started fencing on the pampas. They hired gauchos as ranch hands, bringing order to their wild lives. Today, most gauchos have moved off the pampas.

Argentines today idolize the gauchos. The epic poem *El gaucho Martín Fierro*, written by José Hernández in 1872, helped cement the gaucho legend in the nation's psyche. Young and old look up to these tough men who rejected modern society. A romanticized idea of their independent lives on the plains appeals to the country's urban population.

Evita

Argentines either love or abhor Eva Duarte Perón (1919–1952), better known as Evita. The young second wife of Argentina's former president Juan Domingo Perón, she helped him win the popular support of the poor, called the *descamisados* (shirtless ones). Eva Duarte was born in a small impoverished village. She became an actress when she turned fifteen and had a popular radio show when she met Colonel Juan Domingo Perón in 1944.

Evita helped Perón with his political career, praising him on her radio show as a champion of the poor. They married in

The Outlaws of Patagonia

The famous American bandits Leroy Parker and Henry Longabaugh, better known as Butch Cassidy and the Sundance Kid, lived in Patagonia from 1901 to 1907. They fled to the region in an attempt to escape the Pinkerton detectives. They settled down on a cattle ranch near the town of Cholila. But the two could not resist the lure of gold and went back to robbing banks and mines. They left Argentina in 1907 and ended up in Bolivia in 1908. The Bolivian army claims to have killed Butch and Sundance in a shootout that year, but some say the pair escaped and enjoyed long lives. People around Cholila still speak of Butch and Sundance as having been good neighbors.

1945. Perón became president the next year. When upper-class charitable groups snubbed Evita for her working-class background, she cut their funding and set up her own charity, the Eva Peron Social Aid Foundation. It built schools and hospitals, trained nurses, and filtered money to the poor. Evita died of cancer in 1952.

Evita is considered the patron saint of Argentina's impoverished population even though the Vatican vetoed efforts to have her officially declared a Catholic saint. Masses are still held in honor of Evita, "the Lady of Hope," as she continues to be a symbol of the struggle for justice and equality.

Evita's early death shocked the nation and sent it deep into mourning. Poor Argentines had closely identified with her rags-to-riches story. Distraught descamisados felt as though their only champion had died. Juan Perón's increasingly authoritarian rule and the country's economic problems made Argentines long for Evita's generous public persona. Rumors began circulating that her spirit was capable of working miracles from beyond the grave, and Argentines began petitioning for her sainthood. Thus far, the Vatican has rejected their pleas to canonize Evita.

Death

Some visitors to Argentina shake their heads and claim that the nation has an unhealthy obsession with death. Many of the country's national heroes are remembered on the anniversaries marking their deaths, rather than their birthdays. Argentines think nothing of spending an afternoon strolling through a cemetery.

Recoleta Cemetery in Buenos Aires houses the remains of some of Argentina's most famous citizens and is the city's number one tourist attraction. Plots in this cemetery are extremely expensive. Mourners from all over the world come here for a look at Eva Perón's black marble tomb. The anti-Peronists stole her embalmed body in 1955, hiding it in Europe for sixteen years. Argentines did not want to risk losing her again. Today, her body is buried 30 feet (9 m) deep, protected by bulletproof steel plates.

Argentines were disappointed when famous writer Jorge Luis Borges chose to be buried in Switzerland. Some still hope to bring his remains to Recoleta Cemetery. A similar effort took place to move the body of tango musician Carlos Gardel back to the

country after it had been interred in Colombia, New York, Rio de Janeiro, and Montevideo.

Chacarita Cemetery, Gardel's final resting place, is the largest urban cemetery in the world. It is so huge and popular that visitors can purchase snacks from vendors working inside the walls. Numbered streets allow them to drive to the tombs of their choice.

Carlos Gardel, known as the songbird of Buenos Aires, died in a plane crash in 1935, and his body was brought by horse-drawn carriage to the cemetery where a tomb had been erected. His devoted followers, known as Gardelianos, play his music every day and ensure that his movies continue to circulate. Every day, a swarm of visitors leave flowers and place a lit cigarette in the metal hand of the life-sized statue outside of the tomb in Chacarita Cemetery, shown here.

ARGENTINE FESTIVALS AND CEREMONIES OF ANTIQUITY AND TODAY

5

Argentina's holidays have roots in European tradition, the Catholic calendar, and the country's own folk culture. Feast days are numerous and popularly observed, even if most Argentines attend church only on special occasions. National holidays from Labor Day to San Martín Day mark the country's pride in its history. The fun-loving Argentines need no prodding to turn out for the singing and parades prominent in festivals across the country.

Religious Feast Days

Easter Sunday is the most important feast day of the Catholic Church. Argentines open Lent, the forty days preceding Easter, with a vibrant Carnival. It begins on Shrove Tuesday and lasts for about two weeks. Though not as colorful or chaotic as in other South American nations, Argentina's Carnival parades in the northern provinces are still impressive. Throughout the country, boisterous Argentines of all ages cut loose by tossing water balloons and spraying each other down with fake snow. Maundy Thursday, Good Friday, and Easter Sunday are all national holidays. People who otherwise never attend

A statue of the Virgin of Luján *(left)*. In many taxis, buses, and cars, an icon of the Virgin of Luján is displayed wearing Argentina's national colors and the benediction, "May she guide your journey." By the late eighteenth century, Luján had become the most important national pilgrimage site. During the country's fight for independence, the Virgin of Luján was the symbol of victory. Captured flags were placed in her sanctuary. Argentina's largest festival is Carnival *(above)*. It is celebrated just before Lent, the traditional period of fasting before Easter. Every region has its own type of celebration for Carnival. In the northern province of Salta, people dance the samba and the carnavalito. In the northeast, people sing songs called chamamé accompanied by accordions and harps.

The Bloodless Bullfight

Argentina celebrates the Assumption of the Virgin on August 15. Many devout Catholics attend services on this day. The town of Casabindo celebrates by hosting Argentina's only bullfight. People gather around an arena, where riders perform dazzling stunts before the main event begins. Handlers lead a bull into the arena, where it is challenged by horseless, unarmed men. The challenge of this "bullfight" comes not in slaying the bull, but in getting close enough to untie the ribbons and coins adorning its horns.

church services often show up during this week. Families spend time together and prepare elaborate Easter feasts.

Argentina honors its patron saint, the Virgin of Luján, on May 8. In 1630, a man tried to transport two statues of the Virgin Mary across Argentina to Brazil. His cart became stuck and would not budge until he removed one of the statues. Argentines took it as a sign that the statue should remain in Luján. Argentines celebrate the Virgin's feast day by making pilgrimages to Luján. Many approach the statue crawling on their hands and knees.

Christmas in Argentina takes place during the country's summer. Nonetheless, it is

Thousands of people every year travel on foot from Buenos Aires to honor the patron saint of Argentina. According to legend, in 1630, two statues were traveling from town to town in a cart, which got stuck at Luján. One statue had to be removed, and people built a chapel where the statue would be safe. Today, a large basilica replaces the original chapel.

Italians remember their European origins at la Boca Harbor in Buenos Aires. In the early part of the twentieth century, European immigrants contributed to the development of Argentina's labor movement. Since many of the arriving immigrants were trade workers, they constituted the backbone of the country's economic boom.

common to see Father Christmas spreading holiday cheer in the larger cities, sweltering in the heat under his heavy costume. Argentines put up Christmas trees and other decorations on December 24. These often include lights and cotton meant to represent snow. Families exchange gifts, and Father Christmas pays a visit to children. Christmas itself is usually a beautiful summer day. While some attend church services, others take advantage of the weather with picnics and barbecues. They feast on ham and steak, sipping iced drinks and champagne. Argentines celebrate Epiphany on January 6, the day that the three wise men visited baby

Children at the Plaza de Mayo in Buenos Aires help celebrate Argentina's independence day, Revolución en Mayo. This day commemorates the anniversary of Argentina's revolt against Spain. Argentines refused to acknowledge Joseph Bonaparte, Napoléon's brother, as the ruler of Spain. This eventually led to Argentina gaining its independence in 1816.

Women dance in front of the Cabildo building during Revolución en Mayo. The Cabildo in the city of Buenos Aires housed many of Argentina's early political leaders during the fight for independence. It was here that the revolution began. Every May 25, Argentines celebrate with parades and religious ceremonies.

Jesus. Children leave hay and buckets of water for the camels of the wise men. When they wake up in the morning, they find their shoes stuffed with candy.

National Holidays

The year opens with a national holiday on January 1, although New Year celebrations begin on December 30. Parades are held through business districts, while office workers toss their old calendars and paper confetti out their windows. May 1 is Labor Day, honoring all hardworking Argentines. Some take ski trips south while others just relax at home.

The country is so proud of its struggle for independence that it celebrates twice a year. May 25 marks the anniversary of the 1810 revolution, known as the Revolución en Mayo, that led to Argentina's break from Spain. The country also celebrates its 1816 declaration of independence on July 9. August 17 is San Martín Day, honoring the Argentine hero General José de San Martín on the day of his death.

Argentina's Missing Pieces

In 1982, Argentina fought a war with Great Britain over a small chain of islands off its coast called the Falklands, or Islas Malvinas. British settlements had existed on the islands since 1765, but Argentina claimed them in 1820. The British took control of the islands from Argentina in 1833, but Argentina refused to acknowledge its loss. The Argentine army invaded the islands in 1982 and held on for ten weeks before surrendering to British forces.

Shown above is the Malvinas War Memorial in Buenos Aires, which names the 655 Argentines who died in the struggle to control the Islas Malvinas.

To this day, Argentina still claims the Falklands, though islanders consider themselves staunchly British and refuse to acknowledge Argentina's overtures. They even rejected an Argentine offer to buy the islands. Despite this rejection, Argentina's government continues its campaign to convince the world that it owns the Falklands. Every airport, seaport, and highway into the country proclaims that the islands belong to Argentina. Maps brought into the country must call them the Islas Malvinas, not the Falkland Islands. If they do not, then "Falkland Islands" is scratched out and "Islas Malvinas" is penciled in.

Argentina's most bizarre national holiday is Malvinas Day, held on June 10. This day commemorates Argentina's struggle to take possession of the Falkland Islands (called Islas Malvinas in Argentina) from Great Britain. Argentina celebrates its attempt to take the islands on this day, even though Great Britain won the war.

Festivals

Festivals held all over Argentina recognize the nation's rich and diverse heritage. The Fiesta de Doma y Folklorico, held in Córdoba through the first fifteen days of

San Antonio de Areco, located in the northern pampas, has hosted the Dia de la Tradición for over 90 years. Each November, thousands of tourists and Argentines visit the town to see the country's largest gaucho festival, with its spectacular shows of horse racing, roping, and riding. Visitors can also purchase two of Argentina's most prized souvenirs, *rastras* (silver studded belts) and *facones* (long bladed knives), which are made by skilled artisans.

January, offers folk music and tradition and ends with a flashy rodeo. Día de la Tradicion on November 10 gives the whole country a chance to celebrate gaucho culture. Folk singing, rodeos, and riding demonstrations take place in festivals all over Argentina.

In the heart of the Cuyo, the Vendimia Wine Festival celebrates the region's famous wines. The event takes place during the first week of March in Mendoza. The city's Parque San Martín serves as a center for the activities, including music and dancing. Traditionally, Argentine beauty queens participate by stomping on grapes. The northern city of Salta honors the death of General José de San Martín during Salta Week, which lasts from June 14 to 20. Parades take place throughout the city, and bonfires light up the nights for

A family celebrates Mother's Day in Buenos Aires. In Argentina, Mother's Day is the second Sunday in October. It is celebrated much the same way as in the United States. Argentines also celebrate friendship at the end of June with a holiday called the Day of Friendship. Many people send cards and call their friends on this day.

dances and feasts. The little Germanic town of Villa General Belgrano celebrates its German heritage during Oktoberfest. This gives Argentines accustomed to beef and the tango a chance to sample sauerkraut and hear polka music.

Milestone Holidays

Argentine children typically celebrate their birthdays with a small party and cake. Kids receive presents and a tug on the ear for each year of their life. When girls turn fifteen, they have a special party called a *quinceañera*. The quinceañera marks the end of the girl's childhood and the beginning of her life as a woman. She usually dresses up for the day in a white dress. Friends and family come to a party often held at home, complete with a huge white cake. Sometimes the quinceañera becomes a lavish social event with expensive gowns, photos, and an article in the newspaper.

The *viaje de egresado* (graduate trip) celebrates a student's graduation from secondary school. Groups of friends usually take a ski trip to Bariloche just after the November graduation. Others can't wait that long and go in July, months before graduating.

THE RELIGIONS OF ARGENTINA THROUGHOUT ITS HISTORY

6

When explorer Juan de Solís claimed Argentina for Spain, he also claimed it for the Catholic Church. One of the primary goals of Spain and the church was to convert the indigenous cultures to Christianity. The first bishop in the territory arrived at Asunción in what is now Paraguay in 1556. Few regular clergy found their way to Argentina, leaving the work of spreading Catholicism to missionaries.

The Jesuit order had the biggest impact among the tribes. In 1609, they went into the northeastern territory known today as the Misiones province to convert the Guaraní tribe. They set up missions where they taught the native tribes farming and trades. They hoped to bring the native cultures into the church through a slow process of education and the mixing of native beliefs with Catholicism. The missions were an enormous success, and the Jesuits eventually established thirty *reducciones* (reservations) for the Guaraní. They organized thousands of converts into societies that revolved around farming, craft work, and faith.

Other Spanish settlers saw force as the only reliable means of converting the country. Brazilian slave hunters attacked the missions in 1630, and thousands of people died. Instead of giving up, the Jesuits moved their missions farther south. From there they called for an end to brutality against the Guaraní, but they were ignored. The Spanish forced the Jesuits out of Argentina in 1728, allowing

This is an interior view of the Metropolitan Cathedral located on the Plaza de Mayo in Buenos Aires *(left)*. Completed in 1829, the cathedral houses regimental flags captured in battle by Argentine troops, the mausoleum of San Martín, the tomb of the unknown soldier, and religious art. A monogram is carved on the wall of the San Ignazio Mini mission *(above)*. The mission was established by Jesuits in 1610 to educate the Guaraní people and protect them from conquerors.

Established in 1610, the San Ignazio Miní was destroyed in 1817 by order of a Paraguayan dictator. This mission at one time housed 5,100, serving as a sanctuary for the Guaraní people. Priests at the mission printed prayer books in the Guaraní's language, which fostered Christianity in the New World and maintained local language. The ruins show the blending of Jesuit and Guaraní culture, combining decorative Spanish baroque with native sculpture and architecture. Best preserved are the columns, galleries, and church steps.

settlers to take the Misiones territory. Benedictine and Dominican missionaries replaced the Jesuits but met greater resistance from the natives. The Jesuit mission buildings fell into decline or were abandoned. Today, the United Nations Educational, Scientific and Cultural Organization (UNESCO) has recognized the impressive ruins of San Ignazio Miní as a national monument for its historical significance.

The Catholic Church in Argentina had become the country's most influential institution by the early nineteenth century. The church maintained its power through a system called the *patronato*. Money and favors were exchanged for political support between church and government officials. The system allowed politicians to buy votes from congregations. Bernardino Rivadavia brought the church under state control in 1822. The government regulated all of the church's property and clergy. Rather than reforming the clergy, this move allowed both the church and the government more room to influence each other.

The second article of Argentina's federal constitution, created in 1853, states that "the Federal Government supports the Roman Catholic Apostolic Religion." Although the Argentine constitution allows for freedom of religion, a majority of the population is Catholic. A census revealed that for every thousand inhabitants, there were 991 Catholics, 7 Protestants, and 2 Jews.

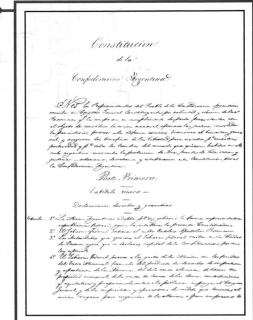

Rivadavia and his successor, Juan Manuel de Rosas, worked to cut the ties between the pope in the Vatican and the Argentine Catholic Church. Rosas wanted to use the church to make his own government more powerful. In 1831, he voided all edicts from Rome posted after 1810, and he put himself in charge of church appointments. Only clergy loyal to his regime could win appointments. The church in turn ensured that its members also supported Rosas.

The church kept a hand in the government after the Rosas regime ended in 1852. The Constitution of 1853 guaranteed religious freedom for all Argentines. Under the influence of the Catholic Church, it established Catholicism as the state religion. It also required that Argentina's president be Catholic.

Reform measures did not begin to take place until after Buenos Aires was consolidated as Argentina's capital in 1880. President Julio A. Roca began chipping away at the influence of the church. He established state elementary education in Buenos Aires, taking the schools out of church hands. He legalized marriages outside the church and secular burials. Argentina also expelled the papal *nuncio*, the pope's representative, and severed diplomatic relations with the Vatican. A growing Socialist movement even began petitioning the government for a formal separation of church and state during the 1890s.

The Catholic Church in the Twentieth Century

A movement called Catholic Nationalism began taking shape in Argentina during the early twentieth century. The movement called for Catholics to repair society's problems by acting as a moral influence. They were supposed to achieve this through

During Eva Perón's grand tour of Europe in 1947, she received a private half-hour audience with Pope Pius XII. Eva was also welcomed in Spain where General Franco bestowed upon her Spain's highest honor, the Grand Cross of Isabella the Catholic. Eva understood that the Vatican and the support of Catholic countries would influence the Argentine people and help her husband gain the presidency.

charity and publications. By reaching out to the people, the church remained a powerful force in Argentine society and a key political player. The church supported Juan Perón's presidential bid in 1946. Perón won the election and fulfilled a promise to enact legislation that would restore religious instruction in public schools in 1947.

The church soon began to complain as Perón's government manipulated charities to increase its popularity while the country endured economic troubles. It objected to the teaching of Peronist propaganda in the schools. In 1952, it also drew the line at making Perón's late wife, Evita, a saint. The church soon became the only voice of opposition as Perón's policies became more authoritarian. Perón accused the church of supporting political opposition parties, and in July 1954, he withdrew legal standing from Catholic activist organizations. He stopped state money from reaching private church schools and reversed his own legislation calling for religious instruction in state schools. He even scandalized the church by threatening to legalize divorce and prostitution.

Argentines from the *descamisados* to the military used Perón's clashes with the church as a rallying point. Perón was forced to resign on September 19, 1955. The church emerged more powerful than ever.

Most church officials maintained close ties to the variety of dictatorships and failed presidencies that followed Perón's fall. Others began supporting the poor and downtrodden. In 1962, Pope Paul IV called for a series of international

Tanks protect the government building during the military removal of President Juan Perón from office on September 19, 1955. Army revolts against Perón began in Córdoba, Rosario, and Santa Fe. The navy and air force joined shortly after and threatened to bomb Buenos Aires unless Perón resigned.

meetings of church officials, leaders, and intellectuals. The meetings, called the Vatican II, lasted for several years. The conferences affirmed the church's commitment to the poor and oriented it toward a position of action against injustice, a mode of thought called liberation theology. A group of Argentine priests acted on the conferences by forming a group called the Movement of Priests for the Third World. They argued that the church and clergy should give up their property and privileges to live like their parishioners. Some eight hundred of Argentina's five thousand priests eventually came to join this movement and began working directly with the poor.

When a military junta deposed President Isabel Perón in 1976, many powerful church figures looked the other way. The bishops held their tongues when human rights abuses were revealed during the period from 1976 to 1983. Some even made pro-military statements, though one bishop and several members of the Movement of Priests for the Third World had been killed! The papal nuncio Pio Laghi, the Vatican's representative in Argentina, assured the world that though many in the clergy were not obviously speaking out against the abuses, they were protesting them in closed conferences. It is now known that many officials inside the church worked with this dictatorship, called the Proceso de Reorganización Nacional (Process of National Reorganization). Pio Laghi himself, later named a cardinal within the church, has been charged for his involvement in the dictatorship's war crimes.

A mass in Buenos Aires celebrates the first communions of young Catholics. Children must prepare by attending religious classes for two years. They usually make their first communions between the ages of seven and nine.

Modern Catholicism

Religious freedom is guaranteed in Argentina today, though Catholicism is still the country's religion. About 90 percent of Argentina's population belong to the Catholic Church. Despite this huge number, less than 20 percent regularly attend church services. The church functions more as a cultural institution than a gathering place for the community. Politically, the church fought the legalization of divorce until 1987. Even today, Argentines are legally bound to register their children with a Christian name upon birth.

Though few attend services, the Catholic Church plays a role in the average Argentine's life from infancy. At the age of six months, a child is baptized in a quiet family ceremony held at the parents' parish church. In rural locales, the ceremony takes on a more festive atmosphere. The entire community celebrates with food and drink. Children officially become church members around the age of eight, when they take their first communion. The church remains present in the lives of nearly all its members through saints' days, weddings, feast days, and funerals. Regular services include Wednesday and Sunday masses, along with weekly private confessionals.

Judaism

About 2 percent of all Argentines are Jewish, but their number makes up a significant community. Argentina's Jewish population is the largest in South America and the fifth largest in the world.

The first of Argentina's Jewish settlers came to the country in the 1880s, fleeing religious persecution in Europe, and established colonies in the Pampas.

The colonies shrank as Jewish settlers gave up on farming and moved to Buenos Aires. Conflicts frequently arose between first-generation settlers who

The Jewish Colonization Association

A wealthy Jewish philanthropist named Baron Maurice de Hirsch set up an organization called the Jewish Colonization Association (JCA) in 1889. Its mission was to send Jewish settlers from Europe to Argentina. There they would establish a new Jewish homeland centered around farming. The first ship sent to Argentina by the JCA held only 824 Jewish settlers seeking better lives. By the time the baron died in 1896, the JCA owned about 750,000 acres (303,514 hectares) of land farmed by 6,757 colonists. The JCA fell apart shortly after Maurice de Hirsch's death, but it had succeeded in bringing a Jewish community to South America.

wanted to hold on to tradition and their children, eager to join mainstream Argentine society. Early Jewish settlers often faced discrimination from other citizens. A strong vein of anti-Semitism ran through the military and government for many years. Many in the military sympathized with Nazi Germany during World War II. In 1994, terrorists bombed the headquarters of the Asociación Mutual Israelita Argentina (AMIA, the Jewish Mutual Aid Society), killing eighty-six people. The Jewish community and Argentines as a whole were quick to rally around the victims and demonstrate against the attackers. Still,

A headstone in a Jewish cemetery. Argentine Jews have a strong sense of community with many organizations that help ensure the rights of the Jewish population. Many Jews speak Spanish instead of Ladino and Yiddish.

A wedding ceremony held in an Armenian church in Buenos Aires. The wedding is one of the most uplifting rituals in the Eastern Orthodox Christian Church, of which the Armenian church is a member. The climax of the event is the crowning of the bride and groom. The couple becomes the queen and king of their own kingdom, their home. They are expected to rule with justice, integrity, and wisdom.

no one was arrested, and many now link the federal police to the bombing.

Today, there are between 250,000 and 300,000 Jewish people living in Argentina. Sixty-one synagogues, five major institutions, and numerous schools serve their spiritual and educational needs. Though few of Argentina's Jews are actively practicing, they possess a strong Jewish cultural identity.

Other Faiths

Members of various Protestant churches began moving to Argentina soon after independence. Scottish Presbyterians were among the first, settling around Buenos Aires in 1825. Members of the Anglican Church of England, the Dutch Reform Church, the German Evangelical Church, and several others also arrived during the nineteenth century. These groups came to Argentina to escape persecution, not to convert Native Americans and other Argentines. More recently arrived faiths, such as the Pentecostal Church and Evangelical groups (the Baptists

A Guaraní shaman wears the ceremonial dress. A Guaraní shaman is quoted as saying, "the shaman learns to pray; there are different prayers to guard against snake bite, illness and attack by jaguar, for sun and for rain. The shaman lives like a spirit and has all in his head, a telephone line to god."

and Seventh-Day Adventists, in particular), have been the fastest growing of the Protestant churches. Today, about 5 percent of Argentines belong to an Evangelical Protestant church. Some statistics show that a third of all churchgoing Argentines are Protestants.

The Church of Jesus Christ of Latter-Day Saints, also known as the Mormon Church, is Argentina's fastest growing non-Catholic faith. The first Mormons arrived in the country in 1925. They established a mission in Argentina as the headquarters for spreading their faith throughout South America. The Mormons built their first Argentine chapel in Liniers in 1939. Argentina now has more than 235,000 Mormons, making up 725 congregations. The Mormon Church has ten missions in Argentina devoted to promoting its religion. Today, Mormon missionaries teaching their faith are a highly visible part of Argentine urban life. Some Argentines are very hostile to Mormons. During the Procesio, the conservatively leaning Mormons were often accused of helping the dictatorship. Even today, some Argentines claim that Mormon missionaries from the United States really work for the Central Intelligence Agency (CIA).

Few Native American faiths are still practiced today. Most of their religious traditions were disrupted by the various military campaigns against Native Americans or erased through the efforts of Christian missionaries. For the most part, the tribes were animistic, placing religious and magical significance upon plants, animals, and sacred places. Tribespeople called shamans knew how to communicate with the spirits inhabiting the natural world. They could work with these spirits for the good of the tribe. Rituals and dances performed at certain times were done to cure sickness, bring rain, and guarantee good hunting.

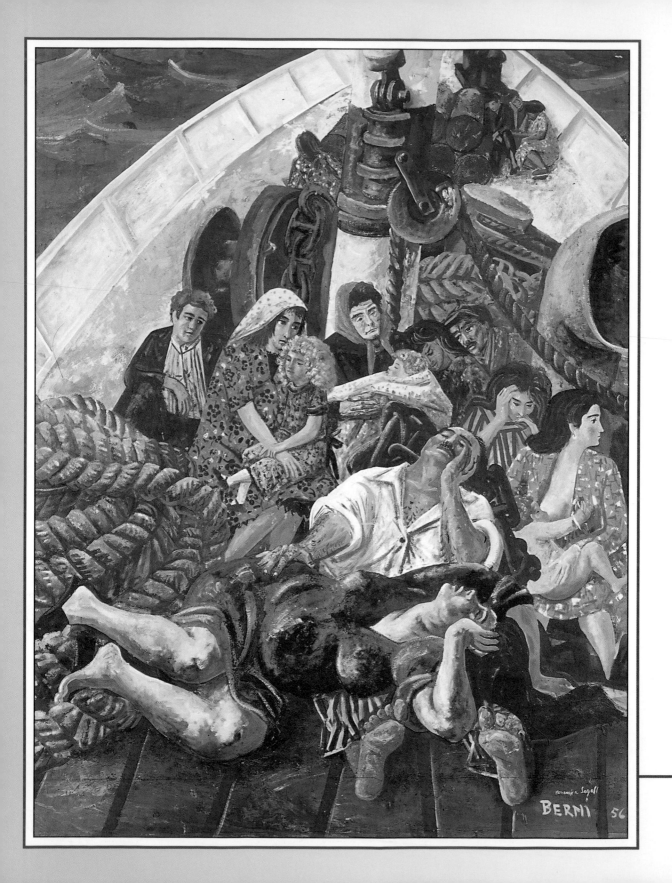

THE ART AND ARCHITECTURE OF ARGENTINA

7

Argentine artists established a unique art tradition during the nineteenth century. Before then, few people in the rough young country had leisure time to study art or the money to commission artwork. Most art served a religious purpose. The Catholic Church decorated churches and cathedrals with paintings and sculptures. A number of early artists came from Europe. During the beginning colonial years, they trained Native Americans living in Jesuit missions in painting, woodcuts, and other media.

Argentines gained an interest in art in the first half of the nineteenth century, after the country gained independence. The new Argentine upper class demanded the latest fashions for their mansions. International artists brought European art traditions to Argentina, and young Argentines traveled to Europe to study with the masters. When they returned, they applied European styles to Argentine subjects. An artistic soldier named Cándido López (1840–1902) lost one hand in battle during the War of the Triple Alliance against Paraguay. Afterward, he painted a series of vivid paintings depicting the war.

As Buenos Aires became the most important city in the country, it also became the cultural center. Carlos Enrique Pellegrini (1800–1875) produced paintings, portraits, and lithographs of the growing city. The most

Antonio Berni's painting *Los Emigrantes (left)* was completed in 1956. As a painter, sculptor, and print-maker, Berni confronted social issues in his work, such as the corruption by the wealthy and the reality of Argentina's lower class. The Avenida Nueve de Julio *(above)* is the largest avenue in the world. The street is twenty-six blocks long and measures 425 feet (130 m) wide. It is bordered by two large fountains and many large, towering billboards.

Native American Art

The first Spaniards exploring Argentina encountered a number of distinct cultures at various stages of development. Some tribes in Tierra del Fuego never progressed beyond tools and ornaments of bone, wood, and stone. Yet they lived comfortably in one of the harshest climates of the globe and developed a rich and complex culture. The advanced societies of the northwest were skilled in metalworking, woodworking, and ceramics.

Native American artifacts date from many different time periods. Some were preserved from the era of Spanish colonization and conquest. Others have been unearthed by archaeologists. Among the oldest are cave paintings in Patagonia, some believed to be from 10,000 to 9000 BC. The stunning Cueva de las Manos, or Cave of the Hands, has walls and ceilings covered with handprints and painted animals. Later cultures produced large standing stones, often carved with human features. After societies began growing crops rather than hunting and gathering food, many began creating distinctive ceramics. These included decorated urns, sculptures, and other decorative pieces as well as dishes for everyday use.

The Spanish invasion shattered many Native American societies, disrupting their daily lives and their cultural traditions. Some Native American art forms survived, and others have been revived as Argentine Native Americans take a new interest in their heritage. Argentines have adopted some elements of Native American art into everyday items as well as in crafts and fine art. Textiles and ceramics bear Native American designs, and weavers make clothes and blankets of alpaca wool.

successful artists of this era followed trends in Europe, such as impressionism, but fused it with Argentine cultural themes. The Museo Nacional de Bellas Artes, the National Museum of Fine Arts, opened in 1896. It is still the leading Argentine art museum today and showcases many fine pieces by Argentine artists as well as European works.

In the early twentieth century, a group called the Boedo changed the direction of Argentine art. Its members addressed social themes in woodcuts, lithographs, and etchings. They tried to create realistic portraits of the working class, who often lived and worked in miserable conditions. Other artists continued to follow trends in Europe. During the twentieth century, Argentine artists experimented with abstraction, cubism, fauvism, surrealism, pop art, and many other styles. The Di Tella brothers founded the influential Instituto Di Tella in 1958. It supported young Argentine artists and brought international art to the public. The institute closed in 1970, due to financial problems and political pressure from the government.

Argentina's greatest artists combine popular styles with their own innovation and Argentine cultural heritage. Benito Quinquela Martín (1890–1977) grew up in the Buenos Aires neighborhood of La Boca. He painted vibrant scenes of daily life in the busy waterfront city. One of Argentina's leading painters, Oscar Alejandro Augustín Schulz Solari (1888–1963), signed his works merely as Xul Solar. His paintings are surreal and mystical, full of bizarre forms and geometric shapes. They involve elements of astrology, mystic symbolism, and occult philosophy. Solar's talents extended beyond

Painting titled *Loading of the Grain* by Benito Quinquela Martín. Using bright colors, Martín painted port life in his hometown of Buenos Aires. Many buildings in La Boca district are painted in these same strong colors to honor him. After Martín's death, his home in La Boca was converted to a museum, which houses his paintings of dock workers.

Xul Solar's painting *Viaje Galáxico* (Galaxy Trip) dates from 1918. Xul Solar studied in Europe where he was influenced by cubists, futurists, and expressionists. He combined literature, metaphysics, and science to create an original artistic style. His paintings have been called "visual poems."

painting. He belonged to an intellectual circle that included the writer Jorge Luis Borges. He dabbled in architecture, created a language called neocriollo, and invented a game similar to chess called panjedrez.

Lucio Fontana (1899–1968) was born in Argentina, although he spent most of his life in Italy. Developing a style of art known as spatialism, he applied this technique to both paintings and sculptures and created huge installations he called spatial environments.

Raquel Forner (1902–1988) was the daughter of Spanish immigrants. The horror of the Spanish Civil War and, later, of World War II profoundly influenced her paintings. During the 1960s and 1970s, she worked on a "Space" series, which considered mankind's role in the universe. Antonio Berni (1905–1981), one of Argentina's greatest artists, addressed social issues in his works. He was a painter, printmaker, and sculptor best known for original collages. Berni visited the *villas miserias*, or shantytowns, of Buenos Aires. He collected scraps of debris and worked them into collages picturing scenes from the villas miserias. Two of his recurring characters, Juanito Laguna and Ramona Montiel, became well known across Argentina.

The architect Luis Benedit (1937–) is also famous for his innovative and eclectic works of art. During the1960s and 1970s, he exhibited habitats filled with animals, plants, and insects. He moved on to a series of sculptures based on the drawings of his young son. Since the 1980s, his paintings and sculptures have examined Argentina's history. Two of his projects spotlighted the voyage of naturalist Charles Darwin, who traveled along Argentina's coast during one of his scientific explorations, and the importance of cattle in the development of Argentina's culture.

Antonio Berni's painting *Juanito Bañándose Entre Latas* (Juanito Bathing Among Tin Cans) dates from 1974. Berni had a lasting impression on Argentine art in the twentieth century. In order to depict the lives of the impoverished in the slums of Buenos Aires, Berni collected trash from the shantytowns and used it in his work.

Theater and Film

Argentine directors have produced some of Latin America's best films. Early films told tales of gauchos and tango dancers. Torre Nilsson (1924–1978) emerged as Argentina's first great director, creating experimental and artistic films. Periods of censorship by oppressive government regimes limited artistic expression in film throughout the century. With the return of democracy in 1983, the cinema began to address some of Argentina's political issues. María Luisa Bemberg (1917–1995), one of Latin America's foremost feminist directors, received an Academy Award nomination for *Camila* in 1984. This historical drama takes place in 1848, during Juan Manuel de Rosas's bloody dictatorship. Luis Puenzo's (1946–) *La Historia Oficial* (The Official Story) won the Oscar for best foreign film of 1986. It tells of a family who adopted a daughter during the military dictatorship of 1976 to 1983. They discover that she had been a child taken by the military from her *desaparecido*, or disappeared, mother.

Argentina has a long tradition of fine theater. The Teatro

Screenwriter and director María Luisa Bemberg's films focused on the challenges that women face in the patriarchal Argentine society. To the right is a still from *I Don't Want to Talk About It*, made in 1994.

The ruins of Quilmes were once inhabited by the Quilmes tribe. Dating circa AD 850, the ruins are located on the eastern slope of the Alto del Rey Mountain. The Quilmes relied on agriculture to sustain them. Throughout the city, they created a complex dam system for the irrigation of the quick draining sandy soil. As their culture thrived, the Quilmes developed a caste system of priests, warriors, and artisans.

Colón holds a theater season each year, and the nearby Teatro Nacional Cervantes also puts on notable plays. A group of playwrights known as the Generation of 1960 concentrated on raising political and social awareness through theater. In 1981, a group of actors held the Teatro Abierto, or Open Theater. They produced a series of plays addressing the years of dictatorship and hope for a new democracy.

Architecture

Native American ruins represent the first notable structures built in Argentina. The Native Americans of Argentina never formed an empire and built fewer impressive cities than societies in other Latin American countries. Groups in the northwest farmed and lived in simple stone houses. They formed small towns of less than three thousand residents. The Calchaquí were the last native group in the area to be conquered by the Spanish, in 1667. The ruins of Quilmes, a principal city, is one of the most important archaeological sites in

An adobe house in Humahuaca. Adobe houses were made with a mixture of mud, sand, and clay, which was poured into a brick mold. These bricks, weighing about 30 pounds (13.6 kg) each, were set in the sun to dry. The adobe construction allows the houses to be warm in the winter and cool in the summer.

Argentina. Farmland surrounded this fortified complex of stone buildings with roofs made of cactus logs. In 1480, the Inca conquered portions of the northwest. They introduced highways and new types of buildings. Tribes of central and southern Argentina relied on fishing, hunting, and gathering. Rather than settling down in one place, they lived as nomads, building temporary dwellings and then moving on.

The Spaniards founded their first settlements in the sixteenth century, but very little early colonial architecture remains intact today. Earthquakes have flattened or damaged many of Argentina's older cities, such as Mendoza and San Juan. The Spanish constructed their first buildings out of regionally available materials. Some were made of adobe (dried packed mud) and had straw roofs. Other settlers built simple stone buildings with wooden roofs. Argentina had very little wealth until the eighteenth century, and the early towns produced few examples of remarkable architecture.

A typical colonial settlement featured a central plaza ringed with a town hall, government house,

Construction of the Córdoba Cathedral began in 1577 and took two centuries to complete. Important Argentine figures depicted within the cathedral include General José María Paz (1791–1854), who fought in the wars of independence, and Fray Mamerto Esquiú (1826–1883), a Franciscan priest who influenced Argentina's constitution of 1853.

church, and other buildings. Many of the first examples of impressive architecture were churches and cathedrals. The city of Córdoba became the center of colonial architectural achievement, and the Cathedral of Córdoba, begun in 1577, is one of Argentina's architectural landmarks. Its creators borrowed many features from great cathedrals of Europe, and it is known for elaborately decorated ceilings and a unique dome.

Estancias can be found across Argentina's countryside. "Estancia" simply means "ranch" in Spanish, but Argentine estancias can be wealthy plantations or small family farms. During the nineteenth century, rich landowners called *estancieros* controlled huge estates worked by gauchos. Today, landowners with large estancias still raise cattle and crops, but many also welcome wealthy tourists.

The Spaniards established most of their early settlements in the northwest. Buenos Aires did not become a cultural and architectural leader until much later. One of its few notable early buildings, the Cabildo, which means "town hall," has historical as well as architectural significance. It was built in 1751, and more than fifty years later, Argentine patriots planned the movement for independence in the Cabildo. Originally, its width spanned the entire Plaza de Mayo, the heart of the city. In 1880 and again in 1932, sections were demolished to clear space for other projects.

Porteños like to call Buenos Aires the Paris of South America, and during Argentina's golden age, they saw Paris and the great European cities as models. The president lives in the Casa Rosada, or the Pink House, built in 1894. It owes its color to a mix of beef fat, blood, and lime! The Senate and the Chamber of Deputies meet in the Palacio del Congreso, completed in 1906. Architects based it on the Capitol in Washington, D.C. The opulent Teatro Colón, covering an entire city block, opened

The Teatro Colón opera house in Buenos Aires opened on May 25, 1908, with a performance of *Aida*. The theater includes boxed seats for 2,450 people and standing room for 500. The dome, seen at left, was completed by Argentine painter Raúl Soldi in 1966 and depicts the Muses from Greek mythology.

The slums of Buenos Aires house 25 percent of the city's population. Made from wood, tin, and other materials found by the inhabitants, these shantytowns have no running water, sewage system, or electricity. Residents often suffer from health problems caused by the contaminated water.

in 1907. Three architects combined various European styles while planning this opera house. It is internationally famous for its nearly perfect acoustics as well as its beauty. In 1936, the military government cleared a wide swath in the center of the city to create the Avenida Nueve de Julio, which Argentines claim is the world's widest road. At one intersection rises the Obelisco, a 220-foot (67-m) spire. The government constructed this monument to commemorate the four hundredth anniversary of the founding of Buenos Aires. Also in 1936, the art deco Kavanagh Building became Latin America's first skyscraper.

Buenos Aires consists of forty-six *barrios*, or districts, surrounding the downtown area. Most have a central plaza, a main street, and shops. People sometimes call Buenos Aires a city of villages, since each barrio has its own character. Barrios in the northern district boast opulent mansions built at the beginning of the twentieth century. Many houses in the working-class neighborhood of La Boca are constructed of sheet-iron originally taken from ships. The residents painted these unusual homes in vivid colors. San Telmo is famous for its lively cultural scene, and for homes called *chorizo* houses. Named for their sausage-like shape, some of these houses are only about 6 feet (2 m) wide on the streetfront. Because there are so many poor people in Argentina, there are many villas *miserias* at the edges of the city. Their residents live in squalid conditions, housed in temporary shacks with no running water or sewer system.

Since its heyday, Buenos Aires has seen the effects of decades of economic woes throughout the city. Many of the classic old buildings are in disrepair. City officials make little attempt at preserving historic neighborhoods through urban planning. Most new projects do not match the beauty expected of the Paris of South America.

79

THE LITERATURE AND MUSIC OF ARGENTINA

8

Argentina has one of the most literate and literary societies in all of South America. Virtually every block in Buenos Aires and other major cities features a bookshop or newspaper kiosk. The Argentine passion for books is reflected by the millions of people who turn out every April for the International Book Fair held in Buenos Aires.

Early Literature

Argentina produced little surviving literature for the first two centuries of Spanish colonialism. The first truly Argentine literary work was published by Alonso Carrió de la Vandera (1715–1783) in 1776. Titled *El lazarillo de ciegos caminantes* (The Blind Wayfarers), the book is written in the style of a picaresque travelogue, describing a trip between Buenos Aires and Lima, Peru. The author balances his descriptions of life in the colony with irony and criticism of the Spanish government.

A wave of books by politicians emerged in the early nineteenth century. Most of these consisted of political writings and histories. Esteban Echeverría (1805–1851) emerged as the most important of these writers. In addition to several essays critical of the Rosas regime,

A couple dances the tango in Buenos Aires *(left)*. A popular saying in Argentina is "If you watch ten couples dancing tango, you will see ten different styles." People perform their individual techniques depending on the style they learned, and their moods. Transcription of Esteban Echeverría's poem "El Angel Caido" (The Fallen Angel) *(above)*. Echeverría's work reflects the injustice committed by the Argentine dictatorship. He was a leader of the Asociación de Mayo, a secret organization that opposed the dictator.

he also penned South America's first short story. Published twenty years after his death, *El matadero* (The Slaughterhouse) shows the brutality of the slaughterhouse in direct contrast to the arrival of beef on a restaurant table. This contrast symbolizes the violence behind the seeming generosity of the Rosas government.

Another Rosas opponent, Domingo Faustino Sarmiento (1811–1888), authored a book that became the cornerstone of Argentine social history. *Life in the Argentine Republic in the Days of the Tyrants, or Civilization and Barbarism* (1848) describes the Rosas era in terms of struggles between man and nature, good and evil, and urban and rural culture. Written as a prose poem, it recounts how the brutal, uncivilized gaucho culture of the pampas grew into a political force behind Rosas. Sarmiento later became president of Argentina, while his book came to influence most Argentine social writing.

José Hernández (1834–1886) wrote the most enduring of all early Argentine literary pieces. His epic poem *El gaucho Martín Fierro* (1872) tells the story of a gaucho who gets caught up in Argentina's process of modernization. A *payador* (gaucho minstrel), Fierro travels the country bemoaning the disappearance of his lifestyle. Threatened with capture by the authorities, he rejects modern society by going off to live with a Native American tribe. Hernández's poem became an instant classic and keeps the spirit of the gaucho alive.

The Twentieth Century

The poet Leopoldo Lugones (1874–1938) bridged Argentina's literary transition from the nineteenth to the twentieth century. The most celebrated of Argentine poets, Lugones published his first collection of verses, *Las montañas del oro* (The Mountains of Gold) in 1897. His innovative style and outlandish metaphors won him instant recognition. Lugones published his first prose work, *La guerra gaucha* (The

Gaucho War) in 1905. *Las fuerzas extrañas* (Strange Forces) followed in 1906 and established Lugones as a master of the macabre horror story.

Jorge Luis Borges (1899–1986) was the best-known Argentine literary figure. Borges began his writing career as a poet in Spain. He moved back to Argentina in 1921 to start the ultraist movement. The ultraists believed in stripping away excess words in favor of short, bare lines. He became famous for his short stories during the 1940s, publishing his masterwork *Ficciones* in 1944. Borges's stories typically deal with the cyclical nature of life and time. His use of metaphor and levels of reality leave his stories open to many interpretations and inspire a sense of wonder within the reader. Though an international literary icon by the time of his death, Borges never won a Nobel Prize, though many scholars believe he deserved that highest honor. Borges addressed different themes than the Nobelists of his day. The Swedish Academy, which awards the

Boedos and Floridas

Literary circles flourished in Buenos Aires during the early twentieth century. Two very different groups emerged to shape the future of Argentina's literature. The Boedo group worked toward bringing about social change through literature. Writers such as Roberto Mariani (1892–1946) and Arístedes Gandolfi Herrero (1889–1982) narrated the plight of the lower classes and conditions in the workplace. The Florida group concentrated on finding new means of expression and exploring new themes. Jorge Luis Borges was the group's most prominent member. Ultimately, the Florida group succeeded in its mission while the heirs of the Boedos continue to hope.

A portrait of Jorge Luis Borges. Much of Borges's work reflects his fascination with fantasy, dream worlds, and a world made only of ideas. While many of his South American contemporaries focused on political and social themes, Borges delved into eternal questions and perceptions of reality.

prize, tended to recognize authors who addressed social issues in their work. Although he lived through social turmoil and a brutal military dictatorship, Borges did not involve himself in politics.

Borges's most famous contemporary was Julio Cortázar (1914–1984), one of the "boom" writers who brought worldwide attention to South American literature. An expatriate who left Buenos Aires to live in Paris, Cortázar became famous as a master of experimental style. He is best known for his novel *Rayuela* (Hopscotch; 1963). *Rayuela* has no real plot. Instead, it describes the main character's search for the meaning of life in seemingly unconnected episodes. The reader must follow the directions at the end of one chapter in order to go on to next sequential chapter. In this way, the book indeed resembles hopscotch.

Although Julio Cortázar moved to France in 1951, he remained active in Latin American politics. His novel *Bestiario* (Bestiary), published in 1951, was a major success, but it was his novel *Rayuela* (Hopscotch) that earned him fame and an international following. In his work, Cortázar offers alternate scenarios to situations, which allows the reader to interpret the book in many different ways.

Manuel Puig (1932–1990) gained fame after the boom years. Fascinated by movies and popular culture, he integrated many of these themes into his novels. His first novel, *La taición de Rita Hayworth* (Betrayed by Rita Hayworth; 1968) earned the attention of critics and readers alike. It tells the story of a boy growing up in the 1930s whose reality is shaped by Hollywood movies. *El beso de la mujer araña* (The Kiss of the Spider Woman; 1976) became his best-known novel. The two main characters share a prison cell. One is a masculine political activist, while the other is a homosexual who dreams of Hollywood stardom. The novel tracks their interactions and their changing relationship, while criticizing sexual and political oppression.

Many of the current Argentine writers address the confusion and turmoil of their country's recent history. Luisa Valenzuela (1938–) addresses the military dictatorship that lasted from 1976 to 1983 in *Cola de lagartija* (The Lizard's Tail; 1983). This imaginative story applies elements of fantasy and myth to the dictatorship. Ricardo Piglia (1941–) also condemns the dictatorship in *Respiración artificial* (Artificial Respiration; 1980). Working with themes and forms borrowed form Borges and Cortázar, Piglia's novel deals with the reconstruction of history from scattered fragments of information.

Music

The music and dance known as the tango is one of Argentina's proudest national inventions. The stately tango developed from humble origins. During the late nineteenth century, a wave of European immigrants settled in Argentina. At the same time, many Argentines from the interior flocked to Buenos Aires. A majority of these newcomers were working-class men. They visited shady bars and brothels after long days at work. Here, the tango grew out of elements from various musical styles. The gauchos from the pampas brought melancholy tunes called the *milonga*. Immigrants from Italy and eastern Europe contributed musical elements from their homelands. The early tango was also influenced by popular dance music of the time. The bandoneon, a German accordion played with buttons rather than keys, became the instrument most closely associated with the tango. The dance borrowed steps and rhythms from the African *candomble* and the Cuban *habanera*.

Men play the bandoneon, an instrument used to accompany the tango. Introduced to Buenos Aires from Germany circa 1865, the bandoneon became known as El Fueye. Players with no formal training first played the bandoneon and were followed by a generation of skillful musicians who centered the tango orchestra around the instrument. The heavy, somber sound of the bandoneon changed the tone of tango forever.

Portrait of Carlos Gardel, known as *el zorzal criollo*, the songbird of Buenos Aires. Gardel's performance in 1917 to a group of wealthy citizens of Buenos Aires began the "Golden Age of Tango," which lasted until the 1950s. During his life, Gardel achieved international fame. He appeared in tango movies, which established his reputation as the world's leading tango singer.

The tango originated with the working class and underworld of Buenos Aires. Many of the lyrics, peppered with a slang called lunfardo, were too racy for polite company. The enticing tango slowly gained popularity and a wider acceptance, but the upper classes still disdained it. Two events changed their views. In 1911, the tango reached Europe and became the rage. More important, Argentina's greatest tango singer, Carlos Gardel (1890–1935), made the tango a sensation.

Gardel brought the tango to respectability when he performed "Mi noche triste" (My Sad Night) for an elite porteño audience in 1917. He cleaned up the lyrics somewhat but still sang about the seamy side of life using lunfardo slang. Gardel became an instant hit. New technology helped bring about his success. Making his breakthrough just as recordings and the radio became common, he went on to act in movies. All of Argentina mourned when he died in a plane crash at the height of his career. He is a still a national hero.

Since tango's golden age from 1920 to 1940, it has waned and rebounded in popularity. Astor Piazzolla (1921–1992) fused tango with the rhythms and harmonies of jazz in the 1960s. The tango made an international comeback in the 1990s. It has been featured in a wide variety of recent recordings and movies. Piazzolla's music helped create a dark atmosphere in the 1995 American movie *Twelve Monkeys*. Many young Argentines are taking an interest in learning their national music and dance.

Enrique Santos Discépolo (1901–1951), one of the greatest tango composers, characterized the tango as "a sad thought that is danced." Many tangos tell the story of a broken heart or of the woes of the down-and-out. They are often tinged with nostalgia, remembering better times. The words, frequently cynical and ironic, may poke fun at the audience or the singer. The tango is most commonly accompanied by piano, bass, violin, and the mournful bandoneon. Traditionally, tango dancers dressed elegantly and impeccably, men wearing formal suits with neck scarves, women clad in eye-catching dresses and high heels. Men hold their partners close

Astor Piazzolla sought to create a new style of music incorporating sophisticated music with the passion of tango. Although this combination came under attack by critics, Piazzolla persevered and it eventually became an international success.

and lead the dance, while women follow their cues for direction and complicated footwork.

Argentine music branches into other genres besides the tango. The country has a strong tradition of classical music. The various regions each have a distinctive musical style. National audiences enjoy folk music as well as *rock nacional* and other popular artists.

Classical music became well established during the second half of the nineteenth century. Hundreds of thousands of Italian immigrants brought a love of opera to their new homeland. Argentine composers produced many operas in Buenos Aires, and European operas often came to Argentina shortly after opening in Europe. Francisco Hargreaves (1849–1900), the leading opera composer of the time, helped create a unique national style of music. Another nationalistic composer named Alberto Williams (1862–1952) wrote symphonies and operas that used themes from folk music. He took an active role in building up

Argentine children learn tango at an early age. The tango has a dark, sorrowful melody, with lyrics that are nostalgic for missed youth and an idyllic society.

The Teatro Colón, in Buenos Aires, is the second largest opera house in the southern hemisphere. It was designed by Italian architect Francesco Tamburini, who imported marble for large statues and tiled the floor with Venetian mosaics. The Golden Room, with columns and 24-carat gold-leaf molding inspired by the Hall of Mirrors at the Versailles Palace, is used as a concert hall.

Argentina's classical music institutions. He opened the Buenos Aires Music Conservatory in 1893, and supported many music and arts organizations.

Juan Carlos Paz (1901–1972) moved away from nationalism toward a modern music style called serialism, founded in Europe. Carlos Guastavino (1912–) rejected such contemporary trends. He is best known for songs about Argentina that draw on folk and Native American musical traditions. Alberto Ginastera (1916–1983), one of the greatest Latin American composers, brought international acclaim to Argentine music. He applied a mastery of European compositional techniques to nationalistic themes.

Buenos Aires' opera house, the Teatro Colón, ranks with European opera houses in opulence and acoustics. It is the venue of both the National Symphony Orchestra and the National Ballet. Argentine Julio Bocca (1967–), now an internationally famous ballet dancer, started his career at the Colón.

Argentina's regional folk music shows the influence of Native American instruments and musical traditions. Before the arrival of Europeans, folk music played an important role in rituals and festivals. Many of these practices have been blended into regional music and dance. The samba, chacarera, and escondido are popular folk dances across the country. Musicians accompany the dancers on guitar and

An early album cover of Argentine singer and songwriter Mercedes Sosa. Many of her songs focus on themes of love, the beauty of life, social justice, peace, and joy. She pioneered the Nueva Canción (New Song) Movement, which popularized protest music across Chile and Argentina in the 1960s.

bombo, an Argentine drum common in the Andean regions. Gauchos participate in *payadas*, spontaneous song contests. The competitors, often in full gaucho costume, take turns trading spirited verses for appreciative spectators.

A revival interest in folk music called *La Nueva Canción* (the new song) took place in the 1960s and 1970s. Atahualpa Yupanqui (1908–1982) was one of the great folklorists and guitarists of the era. He traveled the country collecting folk songs and was forced into exile at various times because of the political messages in his own songs. Mercedes Sosa (1935–), another folk singer, is still beloved to Argentine audiences.

Rock nacional followed the folklore boom. Rock hero Charly Garcia (1951–), considered the father of Argentina's rock 'n' roll, has attracted crowds of young Argentines for over two decades. Fito Páez (1963–) also retains a loyal following. Some contemporary pop groups include Soda Stereo, Los Redonditos de Ricota, Los Ratones Paranoicos, Los Divididos, and Los Fabulosos Cadillacs. Members of a band called Los Luthiers build their own unconventional instruments.

FAMOUS FOODS AND RECIPES OF ARGENTINA

9

Argentina is a paradise for beef lovers. The first Spanish colonists brought herds of cattle to Buenos Aires during the sixteenth century. Their first attempt at a colony failed, but the cattle roamed free on the pampas and multiplied. The herds became so vast that Argentina began exporting beef abroad in the late 1800s. Today, Argentine beef is a source of national pride, famous across the world. It is essential to most traditional dishes, and most Argentines eat beef in at least one meal daily.

The Grand Asado

The showpiece for Argentine beef is the *asado*. Literally meaning "roast," it offers a variety of cuts of meat cooked over a grill called a *parrilla*. The word "asado" can also refer to an outdoor barbecue where family and friends gather for the day to indulge in food and red wine. The men generally watch the grill, and women prepare salad.

Even the hungriest tourist might be overwhelmed by the amount and variety offered by the asado. The Argentines enjoy beef broiled, grilled, boiled, or

A man monitors the grill during a barbecue *(left)*. The people of Argentina consume more meat per capita than people in any other country in the world. It is not uncommon for gauchos to eat beef for breakfast, lunch, and dinner. Argentines pride themselves on the way they grill beef, calling it an art form. All restaurants and diners serve steaks, and the best restaurants have their *asado* enclosed in glass and facing the street. Restaurants also have open-air grills where beef, chicken, and sausage are cooked on a spit *(above)*.

Argentines often douse both meat and salad with chimichurri, a spicy oil-and-vinegar sauce.

Chimichurri Sauce

Ingredients:
1/2 cup olive or vegetable oil
2 tablespoons light vinegar or fresh lemon juice
1/3 cup fresh parsley, loosely packed
1 clove garlic
2 shallots or 4 scallions
1 teaspoon of fresh basil leaves, thyme, or oregano, or a little of each
Salt and pepper to taste

Procedure:
Mince all the ingredients by hand and add to vinegar. Mix well. Add the oil and mix again. Or chop herbs, garlic, and shallots in a food processor until they are fine. Slowly add the oil and vinegar.

Before serving, let the mixture stand for at least two hours to allow the flavors to meld. Pour over meat or salad. Refrigerate unused portion.

fried, and they eat nearly every part of the cow.

You probably want to try a thick *bife*, or steak. But would you prefer the *bife de costilla* (T-bone steak), a *bife de chorizo* (rump steak cut off the ribs), or a *bife de lomo* (fillet steak)? Most Argentines prefer theirs *bien hecho* (well done), but you can request it a *punto* (medium), or *jugoso* (rare). After you finish the bife and feel ready to burst, you notice a number of other meaty morsels served on the side.

Argentines enjoy bits of the cow that many Americans would not dream of eating such as *ubre* (udder), *sesos* (brain), *riñones* (kidneys), *morcilla* (blood sausage), and *chinchulin* (lower intestine). You would also have the change to sample *lengua* (tongue), *mollejas* (sweetbreads), *higado* (liver), *corazon* (heart), and *chorizo*, a spicy sausage.

Argentine Favorites

Many other national dishes also rely on beef. *Milanesa* is a breaded veal cutlet, and *carbonada* is a beef stew with onions, potatoes, and tomatoes. Argentines also have no shortage of delicious options besides beef. In the far south, ranchers tend vast herds of sheep. Lamb and mutton are popular throughout the country and dominate meals in Patagonia. Health-conscious Argentines are slowly beginning to add more chicken to their diets.

Argentina's coastline extends for a distance the length of the United States, yet Argentines have never adopted seafood as part of their national cuisine. They do,

Flan

Flan is a favorite dessert in Spain and many Latin American countries. Argentines top it with a dollop of whipped cream.

Ingredients:
1/3 cup sugar
2 tablespoons water
2 eggs
1 14-ounce can sweetened
    condensed milk
1/2 cup milk
1 teaspoon vanilla

Flan, a popular Argentine dessert that was introduced by the Spanish settlers, is a type of crème caramel. Made with eggs and milk, it is baked in a cup that sits in a water bath, turned out of its mold, and topped with caramel. Made most often with vanilla, flan may also be flavored with almond, pistachio, and lemon.

Procedure:
Preheat oven to 325°F.

In a small pan, boil sugar and water over medium heat until thick and golden, about 5 to 8 minutes. Immediately pour into four ovenproof custard cups or an 8-inch square baking dish and tilt to coat the sides and bottom. Use oven mitts and be careful because this is very hot.

Beat eggs with a whisk in a small mixing bowl and stir in condensed milk, milk, and vanilla.

Pour custard into prepared cups or dish. Place in a large pan on the oven rack. Pour water into the large pan until it reaches one inch up the outside edge of the cups or dish.

Bake for 55 minutes.

Chill cups or dish, then invert flan onto a plate when ready to serve.

Serves four.

Dulce de leche, which means "sweet milk," is a traditional Argentine dessert. It takes many hours to prepare this dish by caramelizing sugar in milk. A thick, creamy treat, dulce de leche can be eaten by itself, as a topping for ice cream and fresh fruit, as a spread for toast, or as a filling for Argentine pastries.

however, consider frogs a delicacy. Visitors with a taste for the exotic can also sample rheas, armadillos, and guinea pigs.

National dishes commonly include ingredients native to Argentina. Early Spanish settlers adopted staples such as corn, squash, potatoes, and bananas. A stew called *puchero* contains chunks of assorted meats and vegetables such as corn, yams, and potatoes. *Locro* is a soup based on beans and corn. Turnovers known as *empanadas* are popular across South America. They can be filled with either savory or sweet fillings and are baked or fried. Argentines grab an empanada as a snack or serve them as an appetizer for a large meal.

Immigrants arriving in Argentina introduced favorite dishes from their homelands. Many restaurants in Buenos Aires have an international flavor. Even in the interior, German and Swiss settlers influenced local cuisine, and Welsh teahouses occasionally dot the bleak landscape farther south. A wave of Italian immigrants introduced pizza and a variety of pastas. Argentines brag that their Italian dishes match anything made in Italy.

Italians who immigrated to Argentina introduced gnocchi (ñoquis), now a favorite dish. Offering Argentines a delicious alternative to eating meat, gnocchi, sometimes called potato dumplings, are also inexpensive. Shown on the right are gnocchi sprinkled with parmesan cheese.

Ñoquis, or potato dumplings, are often the most inexpensive item on a restaurant menu. Superstitious Argentines eat them on the twenty-ninth of every month and leave a coin under their plate for luck. This custom dates from the days when workers were paid at the beginning of the month and could only afford the cheapest meals by the month's end. Diners would put a peso under their plates to show that they were not completely penniless.

For dessert, Argentines might opt for a simple fruit salad or perhaps a confection with *dulce de leche* and after-dinner coffee. Dulce de leche, an Argentine obsession, is a thick sauce made of milk and sugar. Argentines consume lots of pastries and cakes filled with dulce de leche, and they also spread it on bread, croissants, and fruit.

DAILY LIFE AND CUSTOMS IN ARGENTINA

10

An old saying jokes that "the Mexicans came from the Aztecs, the Peruvians came from the Incas, and the Argentines came from boats." Anyone trying to describe the Argentine people finds a very tangled national identity. Most Argentines are descended from Europeans, and for many years they looked to Europe for trends from architecture to clothing. But the country also holds history and traditions in common with its Latin American neighbors. Although it is the second largest nation in South America and relies heavily on agriculture, more than 80 percent of the population lives in towns and cities. Many Argentines believe that a social and cultural divide exists between the porteños of Buenos Aires and the population of the interior.

Some people consider the Argentine identity crisis a myth, and it is true that most Argentines take great pride in their country regardless of their backgrounds. But Argentina's rocky political and economic histories have given the people a lack of faith in their government. Groups frequently stage protests for gripes both large and small. The Mothers of the Plaza de Mayo have gathered every week since the 1970s to demand that the government disclose what happened to their "disappeared" children. In 2001, the country saw massive uprisings following an economic collapse.

People dine at a café in the Recoleta district of Buenos Aires *(left)*. This district has many Parisian style restaurants that serve food indoors and outdoors. Many restaurants throughout the city also serve international food. Since Argentines tend to eat dinner late, dining out is a popular evening activity. People on the streets of Buenos Aires *(above)*. Many Argentines work and live in urban areas. One-third of the country's population lives in or around Buenos Aires in modern apartments. The rent and utilities for these apartments are very expensive and take up a large portion of a family's monthly income.

In Argentine families, it is common for both parents to work. Children are either cared for by members of the extended family or by day-care workers. Traditionally, young married couples lived with their parents in quarters built on to the larger house. Today, it is becoming more widespread for young families to move into places of their own. Family values are strongly influenced by the Catholic Church. Divorce, although legal, is frowned upon by the church.

A sense of insecurity extends to some Argentines' personal lives as well. Many people turn to psychoanalysis or psychiatry. Parents consult psychiatrists about parenting and also send their children for counseling. Buenos Aires alone has three times more psychiatrists and psychologists per capita than New York State. Many Argentines, both male and female, turn to plastic surgery to reduce the effects of aging.

No matter where they are from, Argentines value their families. Extended family members get together for holidays and weekends. Parents usually have only a couple of children and will spoil them to a ridiculous extent. Children generally live with their parents until marriage. Argentina currently has a very young population, with half of all Argentines under the age of thirty. The government recognizes only civil marriages, although many couples prefer to hold a church wedding as well. Divorce was legalized in 1987 over the resistance of the Catholic Church.

Argentines avidly follow the latest French trends in clothing. They dress more formally and carefully than Americans, even for leisure time. Perfectly groomed, they enjoy *el paseo*, a leisurely stroll ideally in a picturesque plaza. It offers a chance to be admired by friends and strangers alike. Argentine men have their share of Latin American machismo and can act irritatingly sexist toward women. They often murmur flirtatious comments called *piropos* as they walk along the street, which women generally ignore.

Recreation and Leisure

The Argentines are very sociable, and visitors marvel that they have any time in their busy schedules to sleep. They begin their day with a light breakfast of toast or a croissant with coffee. Argentines of the interior might take a long lunch break and a siesta, while porteños may grab only a quick bite during a spare moment. Around 5 PM, many Argentines head to cafés for an afternoon tea of pastries, sandwiches, and tea or coffee. Many have a favorite café and will never pass up a chance to chat leisurely and indulge in sweets. Some Argentines might meet for a chess match, others for a game of truco. This complicated card game requires craftiness and quick thinking.

Restaurants do not open until 9 pm, and it's completely normal to sit down to dinner at midnight. Afterward, it's time for *una salida*, an evening out. Argentines might go to late-night theaters or films, all-night cafés, shops, bars, or nightclubs, and stay out until dawn. For many, however, their active social lives have been limited by concerns about money and rising crime and violence on the street, results of Argentina's shaky economy.

Both women and men greet each other with a kiss on the cheek. Like many Latin Americans, they usually arrive twenty minutes late for any social

Argentines always dine amid a lot of conversation, usually two or three occurring at once. This is called *tertulia*, which is the rhythm of conversation, which also includes hand gestures.

The Magic of Maté

Native Americans introduced settlers to a steeped beverage drunk out of a small gourd called a *mati*. It became a favorite of gauchos, who would gather around a campfire and share maté, as they called it. Centuries later, Argentines are still hooked on what is now known as either yerba maté or simply maté. It is made from the leaves of an evergreen related to holly, and contains the compound mateine, which is similar to caffeine. The sociable Argentines often share maté with a circle of family or friends. The host adds crushed maté leaves to a dried gourd, also referred to as a maté, and fills it with very hot water. Each guest drinks it quickly through a *bombilla*, a straw with a strainer at the end. Then he or she hands it back to the host to be refilled and passed to the next person. Some people prefer sweetened or iced maté.

Few people outside Brazil, Paraguay, and Argentina know about maté. But a few health-conscious foreigners are adopting maté as an alternative to coffee. Unlike coffee, it contains a number of minerals, vitamins, and antioxidants.

event. Argentines are very opinionated and can discuss their views on politics, sports, or national events for hours. They also tend to give every friend and acquaintance a familiar nickname. It may be simply "amigo" or a reference to personal appearance. Even names such as *gordo* (fatty) or *pelado* (baldy) are not intended as insults. The most common, *che*, means "buddy" or just "hey, you!" Other Latin American countries call Argentina the nation of *ches*. A national icon, Ernesto Guevara, adopted this nickname as his own. Che Guevara was a revolutionary of the 1960s who urged people to take collective action against government repression. He supported Fidel Castro's regime in Cuba and died at the hands of the Bolivian military in 1967.

Fútbol, as the Argentines call soccer, is a national obsession. Argentina hosted and won the World Cup in 1978 and won it again in 1986—all of which is a great source of national pride. In 1986, soccer celebrity Diego Maradona led Argentina to victory. The dominant national teams, River Plate and the Boca Juniors, both

Argentine forward Diego Maradona celebrates a score during the World Cup semifinal soccer match against Italy in July 1990. Soccer is the national game of Argentina. Argentina has won silver medals in Olympic soccer several times, though it is still striving for the gold.

represent Buenos Aires barrios. Most Argentine fans don't mind flares and fireworks in the stands or even police action to subdue rowdy supporters. But the *barra braves*, organized armed hooligans also involved in drug dealing and crime, make some people think twice about attending games.

Tennis rose to huge popularity with the success of Guillermo Vilas in the 1970s and of the more recent star Gabriela Sabatini. Juan Manuel Fangio, an auto racer during the 1950s, remains a hero. Argentines also enjoy rugby and cricket, introduced by the British. Some sports, such as skiing and yachting, can be afforded only by the upper classes. The country's varied landscape offers opportunities for fishing, trail riding, hiking, and mountain climbing. Argentina's urban population remains true to its horseback roots. Many people attend or participate in racing, horse shows, and dressage. Polo is also immensely popular. Gauchos compete on horseback in *pato*, a ball game played in teams, *sortija*, a type of jousting, and *doma*, the rodeo.

Argentine tennis star Gabriela Sabatini was born in Buenos Aires and turned pro at the age of fourteen. During her career, she won twenty-seven titles in many international tennis open tournaments. She was also the first female athlete to sign a multimillion-dollar endorsement contract with Pepsi.

EDUCATION AND WORK IN ARGENTINA

11

The high-spirited and cultured Argentines are also a well-educated and highly skilled population. Argentina has one of the highest literacy rates in Latin America. For decades during the late nineteenth and early twentieth centuries, agriculture brought prosperity to the country. A strong industrial sector developed during the twentieth century. But today, an economic crisis has hurt Argentine workers and drained funding for education.

Education

The Argentine school year runs from March to November, with summer vacation lasting from December through February. Some students take classes from 8 AM to noon, while others attend from 1 to 5 PM. Three ten-minute recess breaks punctuate each session. School subjects are similar to those of U.S. schools and include

Spanish, reading, math, science, geography, history, music, art, and athletics. Between periods, children spend recess time in many of the same activities that American students enjoy, such as playing games and jumping rope. Students buy their own supplies, including books and school uniforms.

A construction worker at a low-income housing project in Mendoza *(left)*. Argentina's upper class is filled with politicians, business owners, and senior executives of large companies. The poor live in the villas miserias, where they are lucky to work as shoe shiners and street vendors. Between these extremes is the middle class, who work on farms, in offices, in schools, in hospitals, and in factories. A kindergarten class plays outside in Ushuaia *(above)*. Kindergarten is optional for children younger than five. Children are required to go to school between the ages of six and fourteen.

Children attend a computer class. Education is important and highly valued in Argentine society. A new program launched in 2003 equips 12 million teachers and students with computers and access to the Internet. The plan provides one-third of the population with Web access and an educational intranet that offers long-distance educational opportunities.

Most children attend public schools, though few adults have faith in the country's education system. Teacher salaries across Argentina are extremely low, averaging $300 dollars a month. Three taxes were instituted in 1990 to help fund the nation's public school system. These funds have been revoked since Argentina's economic collapse. The government has handed funding of schools over to the provinces themselves, leaving poor districts scrambling to cover education costs. In 2002, teachers went on a one-hundred-day hunger strike to protest the lack of government funds for public education. Argentines who can afford it place their children in private schools.

The earliest schools in Argentina were run by the Catholic Church. Domingo Faustina Sarmiento is the father of the modern Argentine education system. A former schoolteacher elected to the presidency in 1868, Sarmiento wanted a well-educated nation. He passed a law allowing for the creation of secular public schools in 1869. President Julio A. Roca established the first state-run schools in Buenos Aires in 1880.

The right to a free public education was guaranteed by law in 1884. The system has changed little since, though politicians have

High school students respond to a question. Each province in Argentina is responsible for the establishment of secondary schools. Because of the country's economic decline, funding for schools is scarce and the dropout rate is increasing because students must work to supplement the family income.

occasionally interfered with the curriculum. Religious education was barred from the schools during Sarmiento's presidency but was reinstalled briefly during the 1940s to win Church support of the government.

Today, Argentina offers seven years of free compulsory education. All children between the ages of six and fourteen must go to school. Attendance is near 100 percent, with more than 5 million children in classes. Still, some children do not finish primary school, despite the law. Poorer families may not be able to afford school supplies or may need children to help with tasks such as farmwork, earning extra money, and baby-sitting siblings.

Students receive a diploma upon completion of primary school called the *Certificado de Educación General Básica* (basic certificate of general education). Argentina's high literacy rate of 96.2 percent shows the system's present success, although the economic problems may hurt the next generation of Argentine students.

Secondary School and the University

After primary school, Argentine children have the option of entering secondary school or vocational programs. About 67 percent of eligible Argentines enroll in some type of secondary school. Students who opt for an academic secondary school can choose between five different *polimodals*, or programs, which will prepare them for a university education. Polimodals offered include the humanities and social sciences, natural sciences, production, economics, art, and communication. Students spend five years studying at the secondary school. Three years are devoted to basic education, expanding on the knowledge gained at the primary level. The remaining two years are advanced years. Students spend them in intensive study of their chosen specialty.

Exterior of the National University of Córdoba. Because many college students work and attend school, it may take them an extra year to complete their degree. Less than half of enrolled students have full-time status. Master degrees exist only in fields of study where doctorates are available.

The military regime of 1976 to 1983 left Argentina deep in debt. When Dr. Carlos Saúl Menem became president in 1989, he also faced soaring inflation. He enacted stiff reforms to revive the economy and enacted the Convertibility Law in 1991. This act fixed the peso at the same value of the U.S. dollar. The economy grew from 1991 to 1994 and reached an annual gross domestic product (GDP) growth rate of 8 percent. Argentina fell into a recession in 1998, partly because nervous investors took money out of Latin America. Argentine products were also expensive, and thus less competitive, because of the convertibility of the peso and the dollar.

Fernando de la Rúa, who vowed to rebuild the economy in his campaign, became president in 1999. The economic situation worsened drastically while he held office. He passed austerity measures that cut government spending and raised taxes. Unemployment levels rose and consumer and investor confidence fell. In December 2001, he passed a bank freeze that limited the amount that people could take out of savings accounts. After de la Rúa resigned, President Duhalde ended the convertibility of the peso and the dollar in January 2002. The government also defaulted on $141 billion in debts. It was the largest default in history, an amount equal to a seventh of the debt owed by all developing countries.

The peso dropped in value after being cut from the dollar. Workers' savings and salaries lost worth and inflation rose. Jobless rates rose to 25 percent, and members of the middle class slipped into poverty. More than 50 percent of all Argentines lived at income levels below the poverty line, making less than $2 per day. In November 2002, Argentina defaulted on another debt of $805 million owed to the World Bank. By this time, the peso had lost 70 percent of its value from the previous year. In December 2002, the government lifted the bank freeze.

GOVERNMENT AND POLITICS

Argentina's 1853 constitution established the country as a constitutional democracy. Juan Domingo Perón amended this constitution in 1949. The government restored the original 1853 version in 1989. President Carlos Saúl Menem pushed through amendments in 1994 to allow him to run for another term of office.

The government consists of the executive, legislative, and judicial branches. The president, head of the executive branch, serves as chief of state, commander in chief of the military, and head of the government. Voters elect the president and vice president directly on the same ticket, and the president appoints a cabinet of ministers to assist him. Terms last for four years.

The legislative branch, known as the National Congress, has two houses, the Senate and the Chamber of Deputies. The Senate has seventy-two members, three from each of the twenty-three provinces and three from the city of Buenos Aires. Senators serve terms of six years. Argentina is currently moving to a system by which a third of the senators will be elected every two years. Members of the Chamber of Deputies, made up of 257 deputies, serve four-year terms. Half stand for reelection every two years.

A Supreme Court and a number of lower courts make up the judicial branch. The president appoints the nine Supreme Court justices, subject to approval by the Senate.

Each province has its own constitution, governor, Senate, and Chamber of Deputies. Buenos Aires, as the federal capital, is independent of the province of Buenos Aires. Its municipal government is headed by an elected mayor and sends three senators to Congress.

Two major parties dominate politics in Argentina. Juan Perón founded the Justicialist Party, also referred to as the Peronist Party. It still retains the loyalty of organized labor and the working class, although it has moved away from many of Perón's positions. The Unión Cívica Radical, supported by the middle class, evolved from the Radical Party dating from 1890. It is more conservative than the Justicialist Party. In the 1990s, a number of parties including the Unión Cívica Radical Party joined in a coalition called the Alliance for Work, Justice and Education, often referred to as the Alliance.

Voting is compulsory in Argentina. The law is not strictly enforced, however, and voter registration remains well below 100 percent.

Argentina has a strong relationship with the United States and supports United Nations peacekeeping activities. Through the 1990s, it has worked cooperatively with neighboring Latin American countries to support regional stability.

The most recent presidential elections were held in 1999. Fernando de le Rúa, running for the Alliance coalition, defeated the Peronist candidate Eduardo Duhalde. In 2001, de la Rúa faced political crises and an economic collapse. Argentines across the country led protests in December 2001, resulting in at least twenty-seven deaths. De la Rúa resigned on December 20. After a few interim leaders, Duhalde took the presidency on January 2, 2002. Conflict between the branches of government in early 2002 further eroded Argentines' confidence in their leaders. Elections will be held in April 2003. Duhalde does not plan to run for reelection.

POLITICAL FACT SHEET

Official Country Name: República Argentina, Argentine Republic

Official Flag: A white stripe between two light blue stripes, all of the same width. A sunburst in the center bearing a human face is called the Sun of May.

System of Government: Republic

Federal Structure: A president with executive power acts as chief of state, commander in chief of the military, and head of the government. A bicameral National Congress holds legislative power, divided between the Senate and the Chamber of Deputies. The judicial system includes the Supreme Court and a number of lower courts.

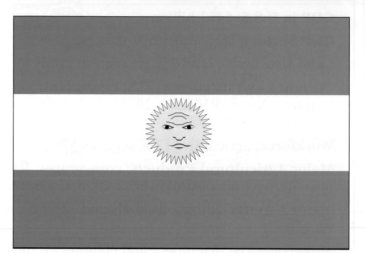

Number of Registered Voters: 24,109,306 (1999)

National Anthem: "Himno Nacional Argentino," adopted in 1813

Mortals! Hear the sacred cry;
Freedom! Freedom! Freedom!
Hear the noise of broken chains.
See noble Equality enthroned.
The United Provinces of the South
Have now displayed their worthy throne.
And the free peoples of the world reply;
We salute the great people of Argentina!
We salute the great people of Argentina!
And the free peoples of the world reply;
We salute the great people of Argentina!
And the free peoples of the world reply;
We salute the great people of Argentina!

CHORUS (three times)
May the laurels be eternal
That we knew how to win.
Let us live crowned with glory,
Or swear to die gloriously.

CULTURAL FACT SHEET

Official Languages: Spanish

Major Religions: nominally Roman Catholic 92% (less than 20% practicing), Protestant 2%, Jewish 2%, other 4%

Capital: Buenos Aires

Population: 36,955,182

Ethnic Groups: European 85%, mostly of Spanish and Italian descent. Mestizo, Native American or other nonwhite groups 15%

Life Expectancy: 75.48 years. Female: 79.03 years; male: 72.1 years

Time: Greenwich Mean Time minus 3 hours (GMT - 0300). The city and province of Buenos Aires observe Daylight Savings Time, but other provinces do not.

Literacy Rate: 96.2%

National Flower: Ceibo

Cultural Leaders:

Visual Arts: Luis Benedit, Antonio Berni, Benito Quinquela Martín, Xul Solar

Literature: Jorge Luis Borges, Julio Cortázar, José Hernández, Manuel Puig

Music: Carlos Gardel, Alberto Ginastera, Astor Piazzolla, Alberto Williams

Entertainment: Los Fabulosos Cadillacs, Charly Garcia, Los Luthiers, Fito Páez, Soda Stereo, Mercedes Sosa

Sports: Boca Juniors, Juan Manuel Fangio, Diego Maradona, River Plate, Gabriela Santini, Guillermo Vilas

National Holidays and Festivals

New Year's Day: January 1
Maundy Thursday: Thursday before Easter
Good Friday: Friday before Easter
Easter Sunday
Labor Day: May 1
Anniversary of the 1810 revolution: May 25
Malvinas Day: June 10

Flag Day: June 20
Independence Day: July 9
Anniversary of General José de San Martín's death: August 17
Columbus Day (Día de la Raza): October 12
Feast of the Immaculate Conception: December 8
Christmas Day: December 25

Working Life: Maximum work week is forty-eight hours; workday is eight hours; any time greater than this amount counts as overtime. Annual vacation time of between fourteen and thirty-five days.

Page 27 (top): Instructions from the president to pirates during the war against Brazil date circa 1825 to 1828. The document is located at the Archivo General de la Nación in Buenos Aires, Argentina.

Page 27 (bottom): Portrait of Juan Manuel de Rosas.

Page 28: Photograph of La Boca Harbor in Buenos Aires, Argentina, taken in the early 1900s.

Page 29: Photograph of immigrants arriving in Buenos Aires, Argentina, taken in the early 1900s.

Page 30 (top): Photograph of President Juan Perón and his wife, Eva, taken on August 28, 1951.

Page 31: Document of the Liberty Revolution dates from 1955. It is located at the Archivo General de la Nación in Buenos Aires, Argentina.

Page 33 (top): Photograph taken at Goose Green Falkland Island at the Argentine surrender on June 2, 1982.

Page 45: Wooden figurine created by artisan of the Guarani culture.

Page 46: Figurines of the Inca culture are located at Catholic University in Salta, Argentina.

Page 48 (bottom): Hand-colored woodcut of Indians hunting guanacos.

Page 50: Photograph of Eva Perón taken on July 2, 1947 in Rome, Italy.

Page 61: Monogram on San Ignacio Mini in San Ignacio, Argentina, established 1610.

Page 62: San Ignacio Mini in San Ignacio, Argentina, established 1610.

Page 63: Argentina's constitution of 1853 is located at the Archivo General de la Nación in Buenos Aires, Argentina.

Page 64: Photograph of Eva Perón taken in Rome, Italy, on June 29, 1947.

Page 65: Photograph of military takeover taken in Buenos Aires, Argentina, on September 16, 1955.

Page 70: *Los Emigrantes*, tempera on canvas by Antonio Berni, dates from 1956.

Page 72 (top): Bronze ax from the Aguada culture dates circa AD 650 to 850 and is located at the Museo de Universidad la Plata in Buenos Aires, Argentina.

Page 72 (bottom): Cave of the Hands cave paintings were created by the Tehuelches Indians. The cave is located in the Santa Cruz province, Argentina.

Page 73: Twentieth-century painting titled *Loading of the Grain* by Benito Quinquela Martín.

Page 74: *Viaje Galáxico*, watercolor on paper, 1918 by Xul Solar.

Page 75 (top): *Juanito Bañándose Entre Latas*, painting, from 1974. by Antonio Berni.

Page 76: Ruins of Quilmes date circa AD 850 and are located in Salta, Argentina.

Page 81: Transcription of "El Angel Caido" by Esteban Echeverría is located at the Archivo General de la Nación in Buenos Aires, Argentina.

Page 82: Portrait of Domingo Faustino Sarmiento dates circa 1870.

Page 83: Portrait of Jorge Luis Borges.

Page 84: Photograph of Julio Cortázar taken in Paris, France, dates from 1982.

Page 86: Portrait of Carlos Gardel.

Page 87 (top): Astor Piazzolla performing in the early 1990s.

Page 88: A program cover for the Teatro Colón in Buenos Aires, Argentina dates from 1929.

Page 106: Portrait of Ernesto Che Guevara dates circa 1965.

Page 110: Note written by Domingo Faustino Sarmiento appeared in *El Nacional*, a daily newspaper in Buenos Aires, on September 14, 1883. It is now located at the Archivo General de la Nación in Buenos Aires, Argentina.

INDEX

About the Author

Theodore Link and Rose McCarthy, who have written many books for the Rosen Publishing Group, live in Chicago, Illinois.

Designer: Geri Giordano; **Cover Designer:** Tahara Hasan; **Editor:** Jill Jarnow; **Photo Researcher:** Fernanda Rocha